AF427825

Love Struck

S E Davis

CONTENTS

one

ORION

My name is Orion Indigo Windwalker, and I have no fucking clue what to do with my life.

As I walked out of the concrete building into the heat of a late-July southern California day, the weight of the official paperwork caused my hand to cramp. Months of desk work, physical therapy, and counseling all led to this shitty moment.

Seven years, four months, and twenty-two days premature departure from the Corps. No twenty years of service retirement for me. I couldn't even qualify for a desk job to finish out my time.

Fuck.

Sign here for your honorable discharge. Thank you for your service. *Oorah.*

Clenching my teeth, I recall where I've been. Knew exactly where I pinged on a map, waiting for a ride out of Camp Pendleton North. I was clueless about what to do. Just that I wanted something... else. Not *more*. Just... an escape.

I didn't want to go home to my family, live in my parents' basement, playing video games between searches for employment opportunities. Multiple buddies had offered their couches for me to crash for as long as needed. Not my style. Nor did I wish to visit the VA for more rehabilitation and therapy.

My plan of career military man puddled at my feet, baked in the intense heat of the summer sun, and blew away on the fumes of a passing car's exhaust.

An Uber picked me up, a minivan popular with soccer moms. I sat quietly in the back, trying not to run my hands over my hair. Instead, elbows perched on my knees, I rested my chin on my thumbs and steepled my fingers. A middle-aged dude drove with a few initial half-assed attempts at conversation—his, not mine. Several errant children's toys from the owner's children decorated the floor and back seat, along with the odor of soured milk. I didn't make small talk, preferring the music of road noise and the jingle of loose change in the ashtray.

On my left, the stables off Vandegrift Boulevard caught my attention. Throughout my time near Camp Pendleton, I never rode at the stables.

Life is baffling. One little thing supposedly can change a person's life course. What was it called? The butterfly effect. A butterfly's flutter affects a life thousands of miles away. Would a visit to the stables have affected my life in any way? Maybe I would have found a partner. Fell off a horse and broke my leg. Missed my last damn "easy" tour.

Leaning back, I stretched out, my calf stiff and my toes tingling. The missing chunk of muscle hadn't been what sealed the deal for my discharge, although it had gotten me a purdy Purple Heart.

With nothing else to do for at least half an hour, I pulled out my new phone to check my messages. I responded to my next stop, giving an ETA. Sent my mom love and kisses. Got a laugh from the meme my sister, Ari, sent. I ignored Courtney's "Call me" text, placing her once more in mute. Dick move, I know. But the girl could not accept either a forward or subtle, "I'm not interested." A slip of judgment during a brief visit home five months ago. Another memory I want to erase.

My pop won't see it that way. Mom? Yeah, she'd be on my side. Always on my side. Best not to put her in that position. Besides, their opinion of me might change after they learn about my discharge.

My new phone dinged, jarring me. After checking it, I spent the next few minutes finding a different notification sound. A simple, anxiety-free noise. Unfortunately, my hands shook so violently after searching for one, I shut my phone off, pocketed it, and took half a Xanax.

I realized too late I should have asked to sit in the front. Nausea coiled and uncoiled in the pit of my stomach while simultaneously pinching the muscle bulge between my thumb and pointer finger. I swallowed hard several times and kept my eyes on the world whizzing by my window.

Shit. I couldn't even handle a simple phone task. No way could I go home. Babied. Looked at with worried eyes and pinched lips. Or worse. Pitied.

I couldn't stand the shame or guilt. Although I know it's not my fault for my mental instability, blameless as those who succumb to Post Traumatic Stress Disorder are. The fact remained I alone am responsible for dealing with my condition. Conditions.

Meds, psychotherapy, and exercise have helped me cope with the anxiety and trauma response. I can't require my family and friends to go through what I have just so they understand. I've been numb for long enough. Getting lost could be the perfect opportunity for me to find myself.

With all my belongings in two bags—a limited selection of clothing, shoes, and toiletries—I still hadn't decided on a direction.

I had always had a purpose. A goal. A task.

How would it feel to have none of those? No responsibility except for myself. At least for a short time.

Mind made up, I let go of the life I had planned—my twenty-year retirement now forfeit. A decision made because of my mental illness. I needed time to heal and seek the life waiting for me. Perhaps in getting lost, I will find purpose.

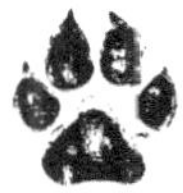

The Ford Bronco came highly recommended by a buddy, Commander Gary Trestle, a POG I met years ago and had been buddies with ever since. Said his grandpa had bought it new, five years before he passed away. His grandma, Shirley Deacon, had decided she wanted to get rid of it. "Why don't you nab it?" I had asked.

"I'm a Chevy man. My reputation would be slandered if I drove around in a Ford. But you're already a jarhead. Only has thirty-two thousand miles." Gary winked when he said it, so I didn't go into the tentative deal with high expectations. He knew I needed something reliable and cheap. Tight-ass Rion reporting for duty. Saving for a rainy day. Well, my last year flooded from downpour after the downpour of shitstorms. Yet, I refused to blow through my bank account for a new car. Gary's recommendation probably had a salvage title. Missing tires. Whatever.

The price of the vehicle was the best part.

The Uber driver, who I hadn't taken the time to chat with, dropped me off without a word. With my duffel and backpack in hand, I walked down a short driveway to a stucco-sided house with rust-colored roof tiles. A little lady stepped out, trailed by a young girl.

"You must be Orion Windwalker."

"You must be Shirley."

"Call me Grandma Shirley." The woman was tall and willowy and had a grip of steel when she shook my hand. Her silver hair hung down her back in a braid. Dressed in tan linen slacks and a billowy white shirt, she looked more *hippie* than *granny*.

"Rion, please. It's nice to meet you."

"And you. This is my great-granddaughter, Lacy."

Lacy, around ten, maybe, gave a shy smile and waved.

"Follow me. I'll show you the Bronco."

Shirley walked me down a neatly trimmed drive to a whitewashed wooden shed near the back of her property. Lacy helped her open the double swing doors.

Inside sat a lone vehicle covered by a white tarp, which Lacy began pulling off. Shirley switched the lights on, and the exposed incandescent bulbs hummed quietly.

The tarp fell away like a prom queen's dress, revealing a gorgeous, sleek form. My heartbeat increased. No way. The tarp hid something that topped any prom queen I ever knew. A '72 Ford Bronco Baja, tri-color paint scheme of Acapulco Blue, Wimbledon White, and Poppy Red. I rubbed my sweaty palms against my jeans. Despite her rumpled uniform, she was still a gem. Perfect symbolism for me. Rugged on the outside, pristine on the inside. Ha. Bullshit, I know, but if I can't laugh at myself, I'm down too deep.

I had to swallow all the drool before I said, "Ma'am? I don't have enough cash to pay for this vehicle."

"I realize the paint needs work, but the body is solid." Shirley scratched her slender neck, just below her ear, her skin and blouse jaundiced in the light. "You think three thousand is too much?"

The girl stood on tiptoes and watched her reflection in the glossy paint of the front quarter panel. She blew a pink bubble as large as her face and sucked it back in before it popped, snapping the gum repeatedly as it returned to her mouth. The skin near my left eye twitched, and I tried not to let it distract me from the horse-powered beauty before me.

The warm light of the bulbs caressed the sleek Bronco. My excitement fell away into disappointment. No way could I afford this beast.

Pop. Lacy smacked the deflated gum.

My leg ached, and I rubbed my index and middle fingertips over my thumb.

Shirley glanced at my hands, then at her great-granddaughter. "Lacy? Go on in and grab Mr. Windwalker a Coke."

"Rion, please." Embarrassment filled the gaps as my excitement continued to dissolve. *Be still, Marine.*

I cleared my throat as Lacy departed, her quick movements stirring up the dust that hung in the air. I was glad when the girl hurried away.

"No, ma'am. I have three thousand. But this is a '72 Ford Bronco Baja."

"Oh shoot. I told you it was something else?" She tilted her head to the side, bright blue eyes intent on me.

"No, ma'am. You got it right. You didn't mention the edition. There were less than six-hundred-fifty of the Baja made over a four-year period. This thing is worth a lot, ma'am. I'd be cheating you."

The lady glanced at the vehicle, a slight smile on her lips. "Let me tell you something, Mr. Wind—, er, Rion. I don't care what it is. It's one less thing to clutter up my life. I'm not interested in more money. You'll be doing me a favor."

Not one to question her offer for a second time, I forked over a pile of crisp one-hundred-dollar bills. And, like some crazy-ass country song, I drove off with a near-priceless vehicle to get lost in the wilderness of western California.

AUGUST

SEPTEMBER

October

TWO

ORION

The ease with which I became lost frightened me. I decided to drive California Highway 1, or the Pacific Coast Highway starting south of LA. In no hurry or desire to cover the entire sixteen hundred-ish miles stretch that extended north into Oregon and Washington. Also, I drove south first, then turned to head north, in the "wrong direction" to get the constant views. Two steps forward, one back. Turnouts and backtracking worked fine for a man in no hurry.

My weekly video counseling session forced a startling visual confrontation of my transformation. No side glance in the rearview or half-assed glimpse of my reflection in Baja Betty's window. I looked... different. My counselor, Lindsey Richardson, asked me if my beard helped with my intentions to hide.

The beard felt somewhat like a disguise, but I liked it. I no longer had regulations to follow. I felt free. Feral. Thinking about shaving it off filled me with a restless feeling and my leg bounced.

"I picked up an armful of paperbacks," I mentioned, changing the topic.

She took the bait. "Reading is an excellent way to disengage your mind and give it a rest. It can be as beneficial as meditation." Lindsey went on about the reduction in hopelessness and powerlessness for those who read. "What about your journaling? How's that going?"

I blinked.

"That well?" She laughed. "Hear me out. Since you enjoy reading fantasies, what about writing your own fiction story? You might find pawning off your feelings on a character will be helpful in dealing with those thoughts that cloud you so frequently."

I doodled on the paper I used to take notes. Her idea held merit.

"Think about it," she leaned closer to the camera. "Orion? You will try for me, right?"

I nodded.

"When you start, just write. Don't worry about spelling or punctuation. Let the words flow out of you. Reread it. Don't. Burn it. Whatever. But give it a try, okay?"

"Yes, mom," I said, tilting my head from side to side. What else did I have to do on my trek to find myself?

"I think you meant, yes, ma'am."

I gave her a cheeky grin. "No, I didn't."

The thing was, I no longer felt an endless numbness. Previous meds had sucked the vigor from me, leaving an empty husk but at least, non-volatile. With some discussion, the doctors tried me with a combination of meds that could give me back some desire to live rather than survive.

So far, so good. The meds kept the nightmares down and the anti-anxiety pills were there to take as needed rather than constantly doping me.

One night, a couple of months after receiving my official release, I found myself alone on a beach. El Capitan Beach. The homeless or vacationers had crowded most areas along the PCH. It was the first quiet place I found. The parking lot had only one other vehicle when I arrived, and I had seen no one else. Hopefully, the Halloween holiday occupied the beach police and granted me plenty of time to rest my sorry ass on the sand.

It was still early, so while not completely sloshed, I prepared to find the bottom of the whiskey from the night before. I sat on the beach and watched the sun's fiery descent, contemplating my own, although without a fire. The dry scrub in Cali had no place for the comforting crackle of flames.

I thought about purpose.

Life.

Love.

I still hadn't broken the news to my family about my departure from the Marines. For all they knew, I was still overseas stationed in Syria. Did that make me a pathetic piece of shit?

Rhetorical question of the hour.

Syria felt like a lifetime ago as I sat in the sand. Earlier that day, I relived a vivid, violent memory in the checkout line at the grocery store thanks to a triggering sound—a whistle. The intense pitch induced an immediate full-body sweat. The sound morphed into a lasting whine. My mouth filled with bile. Had I been able to observe myself, I'm sure my pupils were dilated, my skin red. My body seized, and I tasted the bitter copper pennies as if I held them in my mouth instead of in my hand. The smell of sweet, charred coal and sulfur and shit filled my sinuses and my lungs with each ragged breath I struggled to take.

Lights flashed in the periphery, and loud explosions sounded. The ground moved, a turbulent conveyor that forced me to my knees.

My vision narrowed in on half a torso propped up by the barrel of a sniper rifle. Jagged white shards and crimson splattered across a desert camo canvas. Moist bits of skull, brain, and blood rolled down my cheek.

When reality slammed me back to the surface, worried people gathered and crowded me where I hunched against the candy bar display, shaking like a frightened dog. The excruciating pain in my head now a harsh memory.

A pussy.

No. I shook my head. Broken. Fucked up.

Mental.

PTSD.

I bet they thought I was tripping. Their eyes were filled with a strange mix of pity and accusation. Unknowingly, their sweaty bodies pressed against me, making my claustro-fuckitis worse. My heart fluttered a countdown to detonation. Someone must have realized I had surfaced from my internal battle only to prepare for a ground war. The crowd dispersed, allowing me air and space in which to breathe it.

I didn't bother explaining my former military status, but the short, aged man who helped me up squeezed my shoulder and said, "You alright, Marine?"

Once a Marine, always a Marine, even during a breakdown. Oorah.

From there on out, I promised myself I would become more focused on my health, no matter how lost I felt. Everyone looked at me like, "What a loser brand of drifter." Which I was.

A breeze buffeted my back, catching desiccated leaves and debris and pushing them into the water, pulling me back to the present. The waves pushed white foam up on the beach, stretching toward my bare toes.

Waves crashed over sea rocks to my left and a lone owl hooted in the low-lying scrub of the surrounding shoreline. I stared at the horizon off to one side of the sun, mesmerized by the soft gradation in indigo and violet to salmon and ginger, all shot through by the piercing gold of the distant star.

My mother used to gather my siblings and me in the backyard, wrap us together in blankets to watch the night's advance. We would sip hot cocoa until dusk, then start a fire for s'mores. Mom liked to share stories about her childhood when she and her sister sat beneath the stars. Mom recited stories about their shenanigans and taught us about the constellations and the galaxy. She encouraged us to imagine our own creation stories about how the bears and the hunter came to be in the night sky.

Those quiet evenings were common during the summers early in my youth, even through the mosquito season in North Dakota. They stopped after the incident and I hadn't thought about those nights for years.

Sometimes tragedies bring families closer together, but ours fractured, at least, something inside, my mother had, and it bled into our lives.

It hadn't struck me until then why we stopped our summer traditions.

They reminded Mom too much of her sister. Mom gave up that part with her growing family because of the greater hurt from her first.

I don't fault her for it. Aunt Helen's suicide came as a shock. Out of the blue. Pop said Aunt Helen's death brought peace to her but caused grief and pain for her loved ones. One look at Mom and you knew she felt pounded by wave after tsunami-sized wave of grief.

He said, "Her weakness to ask for help fucked the rest of us for life."

I know now that my father grieved when he said what he did. He hurt and failed to understand the depth and scope of mental illness. After everything I have learned, the incredible complexity cannot be dumbed down into simplistic explanations without creating bias. Mental health is as important to focus on as physical health.

Take, for example, my father's use of the term weakness. Weakness. It wasn't weakness or selfishness that drove my aunt. She felt apart from everyone. Lonely. Wrecked. Lost.

Actually, that's not right. I have no idea what my aunt felt. Weak, lonely, wrecked. Sad. Exhausted. Lost with no other options. Those were things I felt. Things that made me contemplate ending my life.

As I lifted the bottle to my lips, the sun dipped below the horizon, capturing my full attention. My eyes snagged on a green spray of light that flashed above the dropping orb. For a half-second only. I blinked, and it was gone.

A rarity, that green flash.

And with it came the realization that life goes on. I would go on if only to search for more brief moments of beauty.

Life for me would go on, just not in the direct direction of home.

Not yet.

A week later at six a.m., my feet pounded a worn path through the scrub. "Til I Collapse" by Eminem busting me along.

Even though I lived in the Bronco, Baja Betty, I pushed myself to get back into my routine and into better shape. I gave up on the four-a.m. start. Better to run in unfamiliar territory with a bit of light on the path.

P.T.

Regular showers.

Shaving.

Haircut.

The last two I finally splurged on at a slip of a barber shop in Santa Barbara a week earlier, where no one knew me but treated me like family. Freaking exceptional coffee, hot towels, and friendly banter.

I went from grizzled brown bear to military nub in minutes.

When I stood and approached the counter to pay, my barber saluted me and said, "No charge, soldier."

Marines aren't called soldiers, but I let it slide. "What gave me away? The haircut?" I smirked. The refreshing dark stubble crew cut was symbolistic to military personnel in general and felt incredible after the shag I had allowed to grow.

The barber threw a white towel over his shoulder and rubbed his bald black head. "That. And the 'yes, sir,' 'no, sir.'" He winked, the move nearly hidden by his wrinkles of time and smiles. "And your dog tags, son. What branch?"

"Marines." Black tags weren't common, so it surprised me he noticed.

"Me, too. Semper Fi."

Alright. It shouldn't have surprised me. I smiled and saluted him back. "Oorah. Thank you, sir."

"No. Thank you for your service."

I left before I wept, or some other crazy shit happened.

Eminem ended and my run neared its end, so I paused and did thirty burpees on the hiking path, then began a cool-down jog. Returning to my Bronco on the PCH, I found several other vehicles parked around me. Their owners bobbed in a line out on the water for a morning board meeting. I had been thinking about surfing, but I never had, and I didn't have a board. Feeling like a new man, I tentatively placed surf lessons on my mental to-do list.

I pulled my sweaty gray tee off and wiped my face. That initial hump of getting back into shape had seemed as mountainous as hiking to Mount Doom. My body quickly reset into ready mode, though, practically needing the exercise as another outlet for mindfulness. Nothing could beat the high I felt, not even alcohol.

My foot connected on a rock, and I stumbled forward. Correction. A squishy rock that made a high-pitched whine.

"What the—"

A dark lump curled at my feet.

A dog.

The euphoria vanished, instantly replaced by an acute threat response and my instinct to fight. I froze, muscles rigid with remembered pain. Heaving, my breathing became ragged again. My heart pounded a loud, erratic beat in my ears as my vision tunneled. The moths in my stomach beat frantically, whipping up a powerful stream of bile that crept up my throat.

The lump quivered from muscle twitches or the haze of flies that swarmed the creases around its eyes.

The dog looked up at me, blank blue eyes void of hope.

Eyes the color of Dent, a fellow Marine, and good buddy.

The eyes of a dead man.

THree

ORION

I remembered stumbling back from the dog. Away from my Bronco. My lungs burned, my heart thundered in my chest, and my legs felt like lead weights dragging me down. The panic was like a wave of ice water dumped upon my head that sent shivers down to the tips of my toes. I tried a relaxation technique, deep breathing, but no air would come.

Slowly suffocating, I stumbled, and the inflexible earth rose to meet me. I impaled my knees upon sharp stones and wicked outgrowth. Crippling panic surged through me, stalling my thoughts and causing my muscles all to contract at once. The pain faded and left me reeling and lost in a void.

And just like a void, a nothingness, my world went silent, all sound blocked out by the tumultuous beating of my heart. I tried to focus on the rhythm. Tried to breathe.

But then the terror returned with full force. It seized my throat and consumed me completely, filling every inch of space with its icy grip. I felt like nothing could save me from this horrid sensation, relentless and never-ending.

And then I cried out in despair. Hot tears streamed down my face. Cowering into a ball, I felt powerless against the surging emotions, paralyzed by fear and helplessness yet again.

Shadows stretched out into the broken streets; the remains of a once-thriving Syrian village decimated by war. The buildings were in shambles, their crumpled walls dominating the land like a morbid graveyard made of ancient tombstones.

The smell of gunpowder, death, and fire burned the air. A rancid stench, bitter and oily. It settled thickly on the back of my throat like ash. The quiet was unnatural as if the wind had died, but the buildings were alive and held their breath. I sensed the eyes of ghosts, the lost souls craving a return to this violent world, peering down from shattered windows, silent sentinels to the destruction that had befallen their home.

I moved forward cautiously, my sniper rifle held ready in my hands. My spotter, Dent, halted a few steps ahead, scanning the area for any sign of enemies. We had two teams set up in the quad, and Dent and I had come in from the side. We were to move into the far building and settle into a vantage on the roof, waiting it out until midnight, when we expected our target to be moving through.

As we passed one of the few intact buildings, Dent, my spotter, stopped, motioning for me to pause. I followed his gaze. There, in the shadows of the doorway, stood a large Shepherd-looking mutt. The animal's fur, matted and dirt-covered, poorly concealed its sharp bony frame and its tail tucked tightly between its legs.

The sun dipped at just the right angle and bathed the surroundings in the last light of sunset, blood-orange sun rays soon to fade into twilight. Buildings settled, their remains groaning and creaking in protest of their deterioration.

Dent crouched down, pulling a piece of jerky from his pocket. He held it out to the dog, who instinctively moved forward to take it. We knew better than to show mercy or kindness in a war zone, but I also understood that a slight kind gesture could lift one's spirits. I couldn't help the surge of sympathy for the animal.

The dog reached out, sniffing at the jerky, its eyes darting around in fear. As the animal advanced, the light revealed something peculiar on its side, dangling from a rope collar. My mind instantly registered the object, but too late. Much too late. A split second later, the bomb exploded.

The shockwaves blasted through the air, and I felt my body being thrown against the wall. Pain tore through my body. I could faintly hear my own screams over the ringing in my ears. Momentarily, I swore my death was imminent; the shrapnel having already pierced my heart and lungs.

For the longest time I laid there, motionless, until something inside me stirred, some ancient reflex that told me to get up. Move. A burning sensation in my leg began and stole my breath.

The once silent air now echoed with a rain of debris, and muffled voices spewed from my dislodged earpiece. My ragged breathing replaced all sounds while my pulse beat out a disordered rhythm as I pushed myself to move. I found Dent, or what remained of him, propped against the undercarriage of an overturned vehicle. A puppet in need of new appendages. The blood pool grew around him like an embossed painting of hell. I couldn't bear to look, but could not tear my eyes away.

Eventually, a gull's wail broke through the mental assault. The relentless wind brushed over my heated flesh as faint surf noise filtered through my senses.

I felt like puking. A cap of pressure and burning pain encircled my pounding head.

Ignoring my head and swallowing against the rising bile, I counted backward from ten, blinking until I could focus on a rock on the ground. Then I shifted my attention to the grains of sand peppered in the caramel-colored dirt. Back to the rock. Sand. Over and over until my chest expanded and deflated in sync.

Eventually, I lifted my head, my muscles straining as I looked out at the horizon, at the cotton ball-like clouds in a deep blue sky. Taking a few deep breaths, I tried to control my racing heart and calm my mind.

The fear seeped through my veins like poison, numbing me with its intensity. My panic attack felt never-ending.

Once more, I focused on my breathing and on the shapes on the ground. I kept reminding myself of that moment of absolute peace when I first looked out at the horizon. Peace I could find again.

I wasn't gonna let this win. I owned my anxiety.

I scolded myself for getting worked up over a dog. I didn't see a bomb on it, nor a collar.

No.

My name is Orion Indigo Windwalker, and I am no longer in a war.

Slowly, I eased down from the proverbial cliff. Technically speaking, my mind was still warring with itself.

Something soft, like a moth wing, brushed against my cheek, startling me. The dog had belly crawled to me, the sliding track behind it faint. It nosed my face with a dry, hot muzzle, licked it with a feather-light touch, then slid down beside me.

A gray pup with short hair. A stray. In California. Not an emaciated mutt in a war-ravaged Syria. It was small. Injured. Alone. Terrified.

The slight form curled in on itself, barely touching my leg, attempting to disappear. Pathetically thin, its skin sagged on a small frame. Large blue-gray ears. Mournful eyes the color of old ice. Enormous paws. Scrapes crisscrossed its patchy coat.

"Hey, bud," I croaked.

He didn't respond.

Sweat ran down my face. My gut stopped churning, so I took a deep breath and reached out.

A half growl, half moan came from his slight form when I laid my hand on his neck and rubbed him. Loose skin folds moved easily beneath my hand over bones.

"Where did you come from?"

He tried to lift his head, but it seemed to be too much effort for him. The crawl had damn near killed him.

Had one of the nearby vehicles been his ride here? Part of me doubted. It's possible someone ditched him, or he ran away. A pedigreed runaway, though? The pup looked like a Weimaraner.

We were a few feet from my Bronco. I picked up the puppy, cradling him to my chest.

His dry tongue ran over my pectoral, slow and light. It tickled and a piece of my broken self softened.

Inside my mess of a vehicle, I located a small dish and poured bottled water into it. The pup shifted, struggling to rise, so I maneuvered the container beneath his head. He dipped his entire snout into the dish. I pulled it away, afraid he would choke, but the puppy rebelled, a growling whimper demanding the water's return.

I obliged.

He sucked the water down, nose submerged until the bowl emptied. I filled it again until he drank his fill.

A putrid stink rose from him. Of course, my body odor only added to the bouquet. A swim in the ocean post-run would have to wait.

I needed to find a store that sold dog food.

Four

DANI

"Hey, Dani. Could you look at a colicky horse at Vista Nadura?"

"I'm not on call this weekend." I ran a hand through my dark hair, cringing at the oily feeling. Staying up binging on my latest serial obsession on TV had prevented a much-needed shower last night. A colicky horse would stop me from getting a good scrub for a few more hours.

"I know. I'm sorry. But," Stacia, the clinic's receptionist, rambled off her excuses for calling. The new vet on call wasn't comfortable with horses.

I zoned out. Why bother with on-call schedules if we're not gonna stick to them? *Gah.* "Fine. Text me the details."

I threw on my work clothes and a baseball cap and headed out. I needed to swing by Carmel Valley to pick up the vet truck first. Thirty-five minutes away from my ocean-side home just off the PCH.

The sigh I heaved rivaled the most bone-weary sigh of them all. Poor me. I used to have a vet truck to myself. Much more convenient to have one's own work vehicle, that is. I was not an owner, nor did I pay the bills, so I couldn't complain too much about having to share a truck. It was a pain in the ass when it wasn't mine to take home, but not the end of the world.

On any other Friday night, I was in bed by nine p.m. such was my boring divorced life. Yeah, right. Not very boring. I'm too exhausted to do anything other than doddle around the house and cuddle with my pets.

Yesterday, I learned I had lost a classmate. Pissed off more than saddened, I drowned my emotions with a bottle of Syrah and distracted my head with a nineteenth-century romance, heavy on the sex scenes. That Duke—hawt. It's Regé-Jean Page's character, but let's be real. That eyebrow raise was everything.

Ah, well. Off to treat a horse with a bellyache. Fingers crossed it responded to medication so I could get home and get a run in before the heat gave me an excuse not to exercise outdoors.

Within a strip mall, tucked between a clothing store and a coffee shop, sat the clinic where I practiced. Saturday morning and the lot was full in front. No coffee stop for me as the customers lined up outside the door. I parked in the back next to the white Toyota pickup, a white vet box taking up the bed with the Carmel Valley Vet logo curved over a caduceus.

The back door chimed as I walked in to grab keys and check my stock sheet to see if the truck had a refill after the last use. Stacia, the receptionist who had called me, worked the front, directing traffic and phone calls. She threw me a shaka.

The clinic used to be an office supply store, but now it has expanded into two nearby office spaces. There were exam rooms, a surgery room, a radiology room, recovery and holding areas, and a cramped treatment area for dental work and minor surgeries. It was a very busy place. The tile floors were dark enough to hide any grime or blood. A gorgeous slab of polished oak held two desk phones, a laptop, a printer, and neatly arranged pens and notepads for the receptionists.

I snuck in beside Stacia to grab the truck keys from a hook inside a lockable cabinet as another client walked in, the front door chiming.

"Do you think Pavlov felt the urge to feed his dog every time he heard a bell?" I deadpanned.

Stacia let out a hearty laugh, her eyes sparkling with amusement. "Doctor Lavigne, you're so funny."

She'd worked for Carmel Valley for the last three of the nine months I'd been here, and I still couldn't figure Stacia out. Was she genuinely amused by my joke or sucking up? Did it matter?

"Dani, please," I said.

"Only off the clock. At work, you are one of my respected vets."

I huffed and gave her a bright smile, still unsure of her. I acted my happy-go-lucky role with practiced ease. No one liked to work with a Suffering Sally. Was her attitude genuine or an act? "Are you happy here?"

She greeted the client with an amiable smile, her gray eyes twinkling, and placed a clipboard on top of the glossy wooden desktop. The chihuahua in his arms shook like a wet rat, its ears twitching as the man murmured reassuring words.

"I am." Her smile seemed sincere, but then, didn't mine? "This place is busy, but everyone has been great. The clients are kind. I get to see a lot of birds, too."

They were my specialty. The birds and horses. I saw other small animals, cattle, and goats, but horses and birds were my favorites to handle and treat.

"You are welcome to come hang out at my place. I have three resident squawkers you can hang out with."

If her face lit up more, I'd have to put on sunglasses. Was she tearing up? Shit, was I? I glanced away and focused on the shivering chihuahua attempting to climb into his owner's chest.

"That would be amazing. Thank you, Dani. Doctor—"

"Doc is fine. Dani is fine. I gotta run. Keep smiling, Stacia."

"Sorry again for ruining your Saturday off," she offered as I turned to leave.

I waved her apology away. "Don't worry about it. I'm not." And I wasn't. Worried, I mean. I knew going into veterinary medicine would not be a job, but a lifestyle.

My life felt like a rollercoaster, with g-forces pulling from multiple directions. Whenever my phone would ring, my stomach sank with dread for yet another call demanding more of me despite already having overworked myself beyond exhaustion.

And as if on cue, my phone rang while I pulled back onto the PCH.

I had in the past contemplated how easy it would be to step off the figurative rollercoaster. Not turn the corner and take the long drop off a steep cliff to a wet exit. To give into the abyss and let its darkness take me away from this frenzied world. But I knew deep down that a true death wish wasn't something I wanted for myself. Despite all the chaos of my past, I still held onto some hope that one day, I would find what I was looking for. I'm in the dark about what it could be.

I work almost all the time, and when I'm not, I take care of my pets.

I don't want to hurt anyone else. Despite everything, I'm happy I didn't give up. What doesn't kill you makes you stronger, right? Or gets you on meds to help you cope with your shit.

But for the ever love of Jesus, Mary, Luke, and John, who the FUCK was calling me now?

Without glancing at the number, I answered. "Hello." A bit on the gruff side, but sleep deprivation nipped at my heels.

No one responded. My eyes traveled to my phone, docked responsibly on the dash. A Wisconsin area code?

My skin tingled as if a phantom traced my spine with icy fingertips and nails filed into sharp points. A wave of nausea swept away my bravado, and I slowly steered onto the narrow shoulder, praying that no one would crash into me.

He found me.

Cars zoomed by, screeching their horns in protest at the disruption of their smooth ride. I knew I had no right to take up space on that stretch of road, but I took a chance.

He found me.

I hit the end icon and unbuckled the too-tight strap. Then rolled the windows down to allow air inside. Off to my right, the Pacific Ocean glinted like a rolling bed of sapphire, tourmaline, and aquamarine gemstones. Meanwhile, anxiety clamped her claws around me.

He. Found. Me.

Fuck fuck *FUCK*.

The contents of my purse spilled over the bench seat as I searched for my meds. My hands shook violently, but I managed not to spill the pills all over.

I dry swallowed my tablet and called my father.

"Daddy, he found me."

FIVE

ORION

Nothing that happens in life is a simple chance.

That statement has nothing to do with the Marines, but rather, a creation of my own. A recent epiphany. I got lost, searching for a sign. Something to give me direction.

I literally stumbled over the one thing that saved my sorry ass.

Thor.

I found the nearest pet supply store and bought the works, then found a veterinarian clinic that would see us as a walk-in.

My old man used to say there's nothing so impressive as a man in uniform. The embodiment of strength and honor. Mom would smile and agree, then add, "Unless the man holds a puppy he saved from a burning building."

Burning building aside, good thing I had a puppy since my uniform was no longer something I would probably ever wear again.

Regardless of the "why" the veterinary clinic eagerly accepted my walk-in request for a visit, they treated us with respect. Thor's popularity, far higher than my own, climbed when they learned how I found him.

We were called into a room, and I placed Thor on the stainless steel table. Soft music played from hidden speakers and funky, brightly colored animals in various mid-jump poses decorated the ivory walls. The pig in a blue tutu licking at a brown and pink bumblebee drew my attention while the hair on my left forearm drew Thor's. Or it could have been my freckles.

The vet, Dr. Christine, entered with a smile. I pegged her to be in her thirties, her blond hair pulled back into a high ponytail. Silver paw prints adorned her ears, matching the dark blue scrub top with silver paw and nose prints. She introduced herself, offering a brief, firm handshake, then turned her full attention to Thor. During the thorough physical, he took the thermometer up his bum like a champ but got in a few tongue punches to her eyes and one ear, so I guess they had a tie. I gave her extra points for not wrinkling her nose at his noxious aroma.

Because of his malnourished condition, she treated him for parasites and recommended a special shampoo for his skin.

"He looks to be four months old." She lifted Thor's lips and pointed to his incisors. "See these two are adult teeth. His canines haven't poked through. We could give him vaccinations, but you should get him back in a couple of weeks for a booster to be on the safe side." She chewed on her lip. "How long have you had him?"

"Found him after my run this morning."

She eyed me briefly, then returned her focus to the increasingly energetic pup. "Well, it would be wise to be cautious and treat him as a rabies suspect, even though these gashes and cuts are days old and look more like road rash than animal bites."

"An ounce of prevention is worth a pound of cure?" I suggested.

She continued to chew the inside of her lip. "Or death, as is the result with rabies. If his mentality deteriorates, kennel him and notify me immediately."

"I've been vaccinated for rabies." Special ops received a plethora of vaccinations. Theoretically, I should survive almost any disease outbreak, even ones that haven't happened yet.

"Really? Well, in that case, your risk is lower." Dr. Christine clicked her tongue and picked Thor up, nuzzling the little guy. Thankfully, she didn't ask questions about why some bum off the street had a rabies titer.

Either she didn't have a sense of smell, or he tugged at her heartstrings as strongly as Thor did mine. She rattled off the signs to look for that might result from the deadly viral infection in dogs.

"Yes, ma'am."

"Well, you're not southern, I can tell by your accent. Either your mother was strict or you're in the military."

I genuinely smiled. "My momma is strict, and both my parents are military." I skipped my own failed career.

Her keen eyes took me in. "Thank you for your service. If you have time, we can give Thor a bath. Clean his ears. Trim his nails?"

Man, she hit the bonus with that comment. "Yes, ma'am. That would be great." His sharp nails were not malnourished.

"Okay. Would you like to come back with me?"

I had never been in the bowels of a vet clinic before, and my curiosity jumped up and down like a little kid for candy. I easily contained any outward reaction. No need to turn maniacal on these kind people. "Yes, ma'am. Thank you."

Dr. Christine smiled, and I followed her down a short hall and into a large, open room. Five other humans occupied the area with three animals, all dogs.

The disinfectant smell in the clinic was surprisingly like a human hospital with a hint of animal odor mixed in. So long as I didn't catch a whiff of blood, I might stay on my feet during the visit.

"We treat the cats in a separate area." She pointed to the left, past a large window. "That's our surgery suite. That door there leads to the kennels. Here's our employee lounge. It's messy, but you can grab yourself a soda from the fridge. And April brought cupcakes."

"Try the cupcakes. They're a bite of heaven," called one woman working on the south end of a north-facing pit bull.

"One bite?" her partner, a short, gray-haired man, laughed. "Figures you would only need one bite with that big mouth."

The woman stuck her tongue out and the pit bull's backside shook as she wagged her tail. In agreement or blatant happiness?

Dr. Christine said, "Definitely help yourself to the cupcakes. We'll be over there." She gestured with her head to an open sink table, Thor doing his best to lick the top layer of skin from her neck.

One hour later, two cupcakes and a Dt. Coke fuller, several hundred of the best dollars I ever spent shorter, Thor, and I left. He smelled fabulous, had a rabies tag hanging from his new camo collar, and a bag of new puppy treats, samples, shampoo, topical meds, and an oral antiparasitic. And an extra cupcake.

I swung through a drive-through restaurant, grabbing a double-double, animal style.

In the parking lot, I cracked open a can of soft food the vet had recommended to put weight on my boy. With a tongue depressor, also courtesy of the vet, I scooped out food to feed Thor on the seat beside me. He nibbled daintily, like he held an audience with a queen.

I ate my hamburger, mourned its quick disappearance, and continued feeding small bits to Thor.

A song on the radio got me thinking about home. I still hadn't called my family to tell them of my early military departure. They didn't even know about my injury. The longer I waited, the worse the downfall. But maybe there was something that could make it less harsh. What, I did not know.

As I mentioned to Dr. Christine, both my parents were military. Career martial. My parents met in basic. Mom and Dad met, and bam! Love at first sight, they said. Dad's Hispanic, Mom's Irish-German. I am a third-generation military. My brother and sister—also in the service. Marine and Navy. They should understand. Support and understand.

And yet...

Thor's paw on my wrist paused my train of thought.

I swallowed. "What, boy?"

He cocked his head, then jutted his chin up and licked his lips. His gangly body wiggled as he sat. *Aroo.* He bit at the empty tongue depressor—that had just come out of my mouth.

Feeding Thor from his soft canned food while I ate a sandwich had been a mistake. My mind briefly forgot its tasks, and I spooned high-fat, wet puppy chow into my mouth. I moved my tongue around my mouth, scoping out the bits stuck in my cheeks.

I wouldn't say it was the worst I ever ate, but... Once on a dare from my older brother, I consumed an entire C-Rat from a stash we found of my granddad's. Ham, beans and rice, crackers and peanut butter, and a brownie. Ever eat a forty-year-old irradiated brownie?

The puppy food tasted better. Although I spat it out as soon as I realized what I had done.

Thor gobbled it up and licked my mouth and chin clean for good measure.

After a grocery and supply run at Wally World, I cleaned out my Bronco and set it up in style, with a sleeping pad for me and a furry memory foam bed for my partner. Food, water, chew toys, a blue rubber ball, and a red Frisbee rounded out my cache. Since I was spending money, I might as well have a few frivolous things to keep us entertained. My new buddy and I headed for the hills. Literally. I decided we would get away, take in the great outdoors away from crowds and cities.

Thor needed time to mend.

<h1 style="text-align:center">SIX</h1>

<h1 style="text-align:center">DANI</h1>

I hated how I reverted to my youth when faced with the demon who desecrated a good chunk of my recent past. Wasn't it enough that he invaded my dreams, churning them into nightmares that made me wonder if I would ever find someone who could accept my brokenness? Now he had to violate court orders and harass me?

My father, Dr. Gavin Lavigne, had the smooth, steady resolve of a glacier. Strong and supportive, the man gave me opportunities I would not have had with my birth mother. While he soothed my raw wounds with words, my mom, Ariadne Creswell, also a formidable force, soothed them with action. Unfortunately, neither were there to physically comfort me and at that moment, I wanted nothing less than to drown in their hugs.

"Your mom is contacting the detective, sunshine. What can I do?" Dad said, his low voice eased the tension in my spine.

"Do I need to get a new phone number?" The thought of such a change and the hassle it would cause made me cringe. I chewed on my thumbnail. Biting down helped me focus on the now.

He sighed. "Yes. I'll call to get one set—"

"Dad, it's fine. I'll call. I have my afternoon—"

"Which you should spend distracting yourself in other ways besides chewing your nails."

I tugged my thumbnail from my mouth and stuck my tongue out. The fresh ocean breeze brushed my skin. I closed my eyes and listened to the waves crash up the rocky shoreline, my mind trying to relax amidst the barrage of what-ifs.

"Yeah. Okay. Thank you."

"No problem, sunshine. Don't be surprised if one of your brothers stops by."

"Only if they bring the whole family." My eyes teared up. How could I be so lucky with my family, but suck so badly with work and my marriage? Ex-marriage.

As I wallowed in my past mistake of not reading the red flags for what they were, a text came through from a friend.

Right. Back to life. He might have discovered my number. But that's all. I opened the message from my best friend throughout college and veterinary school, Katey Best.

Wtf. Karolina committed suicide. How is her obit not a glorification of a vet with a complete lack of boundaries and a fuck all work-life balance?

She attached a link to an obituary. Dr. Karolina Ford's obituary. She didn't just leave this world; she took her own life. I took a long minute to read it.

Karolina and I hadn't hung in the same circles, but I remembered her well. Those who go to veterinary school, the excited people you share classes and labs with... there is a special bond forged through blood, sweat, tears, dog shit, and horse reflux. A forever connection. Like a coven of witches with your own brand of magic and wacky, diabolical humor. You remember each other. She started with a focus on feline medicine and graduated with an emphasis on dairy. Last I knew, she was in a lucrative practice down south in Alta Dena.

I pressed a clammy palm to my face. The eulogy included phrases like: "She was always available..." "Always smiling..." "Funny, big heart..." "Gave everything for her patients..."

She gave everything, all right. Including her life. The irony of giving up my free Saturday morning wasn't lost upon me, and it took everything to ignore the rising sensations. Anger. Guilt. Shame. Sadness. The key ingredients for Self-Destructing Madness. All it required was a dose of undivided surrender. My internal focus caught on the shadowed figure crumpled in a desolate corner of my mind.

I wanted to shelter that part of me, keep her hydrated and tucked away in the quiet.

Keep going, don't fucking give up.

A hollowness bloomed in my chest, a demanding weight pressing against my sternum. I licked my lips, wanting, no, needing to hear Katey's voice. Before I called her, I pressed my fingertips to the beating pulse on my inner arm, struggling to find it beneath the scar tissue. As I stared off into the horizon, I absently traced the curving lines of the ink that decorated my inner wrist. I wanted to crawl into my bed, beneath my down comforter, and get lost in the darkness and goose musk.

But I couldn't. Not yet.

It took all the strength I could muster to lift a finger to hit the call button. Despite that, I hesitated longer than necessary, allowing more than one vehicle to go by before I pulled back onto the highway.

Katey answered on the fourth ring. "Hey, Dani California!"

Hearing her voice damn near broke me. "Hey, Bear. How are ya?" My eyes not only welled but overflowed.

"I'm a fucking mess. You?"

I sniffed. "Same."

"Yeah, well, prepare to get salty." Katey went off on a verbal rampage about the wonderful profession we dedicated our lives to. "Devotion is so much different from sacrificing our lives, for fuck's sake. When will we learn the job is a J. O. B. The *throw all one's energy into saving lives and making clients happy* mentality should not be revered and emulated? When the fuck will all the people who teach vet med grind it into students that if you love animals, quit vet school? Instead, go into a field that pays you enough you can donate time and money to a shelter?"

Veterinary medicine training, at least when I went to school, glossed over how the inability to say no and set healthy boundaries will have a severely negative impact on mental health. Actually, that was more the responsibility of the parents of all those students, mine included. At least mine make enough for their excess work to be worth it. The "old ways" of doing things in veterinary practice have gotten harder with more and more clients, more debt, more sophistication, and more demands. Setting the standard that we as veterinarians must be exceptional at everything we do is the shovel that we dig our graves with.

Clients, and let's face it, veterinarians, were adept at emotional black-mail, trying to get services cheaper for the former and thinking we should provide it regardless of the cost to save the animals for the latter.

Katey and I, as much as our bitching sessions leaned toward honesty, failed to follow our own sensibilities. We were both run ragged.

"How's that working out for you?" I asked, slowing as my drive came into view. My relief at being home momentarily lapsed into a panic until I pulled up my security feed. Chewing on the inside of my cheek, I reviewed the feed. Nothing out of the ordinary. I hit the clicker for my metal gate and waited patiently for it to open.

"About as well as you. We are down a vet. Again."

"Same. I'm just rolling in from a colic on my weekend off."

"One colic?"

"Uh-huh."

"Lucky. I had two colics and an eye this morning. You're so lame." Katey worked in the northwestern portion of the greater L.A. area. She had a massive ER list compared to mine.

"Next time you're off, pack up your board and come up. Can't answer your phone when you're out on the waves." I mean, you could, but you'd be a dumbshit.

"Oh, baby girl, I totally would if," she paused, the dramatic bitch, "I could bring my cat."

"Um, yeah? Fellow vet and animal lover, here."

I missed Katey. She saved my sorry ass not so long ago, sheltering me when my world fell apart. I couldn't ever thank her enough or pay her back in this life, but I sure as hell would try.

We made retreat plans for the following weekend. Then she had to go. Called away for a laceration. I wished her luck.

"Luck? No luck involved when you can suture like a quilter for the gods."

"And have the humility of a narcissist. Love you, Katey-Bear."

She laughed. "Love you more, Dani California."

The alarm code said, "Welcome," in its feminine electronic voice as I let myself into my home. Bunnie, my Maine Coon cat, sauntered around the corner.

"Hello, baby. How's my big boy?" I held my arms out, and he jumped into them. I buried my face into his luxurious, dark mane, happy to have this incredible creature greet me. He was so freaking good, better than a partner. Never complained about what I fed him. Didn't leave the toilet seat up. Made very few messes. Pushed for affection when I needed com-fort. Snuggled without expecting sex. He shed long black hair everywhere, but since he didn't bitch about my hair clots in the tub, I overlooked him clogging the robotic vacuums.

From the onset, people focusing on a career in veterinary medicine have a tendency toward perfectionism. We have to. Perfect grades placed you in the running. For extra points, we had to be: Top-notch workers (usually cleaning dog runs and cat cages at vet clinics for tiny paychecks). Volunteers for shelters or practice experience. Be leaders in pre-vet clubs. Sign on for high credit loads to prep for veterinary school. The low number of schools makes pushing oneself key in order to outshine the heavy competition.

Once you've mastered it, it's ingrained. We push harder and harder until there isn't any more push left. The harsh plummet back to reality finds some of us reassessing and readjusting our expectations. Others, like Karolina, are driven so deeply underground that there is no return.

I paused my cleaning in the kitchen, a quick wash of my breakfast dishes, to run a thumb over my latest tattoo on the inside of my wrist. A semicolon offset enough to draw one's eyes away from the mostly invisible scar tissue.

I understood the fall and landing more than most, but the practice of veterinary medicine doesn't get to claim full rights to my almost demise. Nor do my tendencies to excel at everything.

Sometimes awful shit happens. I'm not the first person to have been in an abusive relationship. Nor am I someone with the worst cautionary tales. Although only months separated me from my last necessary interaction with *him*, it seemed *he* was not content to abide by the protective order and leave me in peace. Nope. Why had I expected the asshole to allow me time to lick my wounds and heal?

With that last thought, I checked my security system and locked myself and Bunnie in the bird room for some R&R.

seven

DANI

Three weeks passed by without a mysterious call. Katey bailed on our get-together, but her sister had her first baby several weeks prematurely, so she got a pass. I looked forward to a quiet night for once after one more emergency to finish up.

A lab-pittie mix puppy, Eddy, had developed a severe case of oral fixation upon a jug of antifreeze. The owners came home from working their late shifts and found him. They called me and rushed him in.

Now I had a loud drunk mutt in the kennel. At first, his yowling and yodeling were pitifully adorable. They merged into a string of inconsolable sounds that he couldn't help. He was drunk, and all because of the treatment, which included an I.V. infusion of Everclear to counteract the acute poisoning.

His howls pierced my heart at first, but as time passed and they continued on a never-ending loop, a screaming run with both my hands clasped over my bleeding ears out of the clinic sounded perfect. Unfortunately, I had to wait until Gary came in for early rounds. Thanks and prais-es to him, an experienced technician. In the vet field for one-hun-dred-fifty-two years, he looked a day over "don't ask" age.

Five a.m. rolled around. I checked once more on Eddy, my pissed-up puppy. Totally zoned out, he sprawled on the comfy bed his owner brought him. I reached in to nab a towel Eddy had somehow gotten ahold of and bunched it into a ball.

As I stood, Gary came in, all sunshine during the dark morning hours.

"Dani, my darlin', what have you got for me?"

I waved a hand at Eddy and explained. As I spoke, I pressed the towel against my belly. Something cool and wet soaked into my camo scrub top. The ammonia odor tipped me off.

Great. Dog pee.

"Ich. I gotta shower now," I said.

"Hey, one less thing to do when you get home."

Not sure how that differed from one more thing to do at work, but I went with it. Eddy beat me with age and experience.

Deciding on a quick shower before I headed home, I restocked the work truck, then hopped in my Mini. Grabbed a quick caffeine fix at a drive-thru coffee shop on my way out of town and hit the road.

As I drove, I listened to a podcast about women who had overcome similar obstacles to mine in their lives and were learning to trust them-selves again.

Trust. What a hard thing to learn. Even harder to unlearn suspicion and fear.

Instead, I decided to start with bravery and face the truth that what I had experienced wasn't entirely my fault. Regret wasn't a wand I could swish and change anything. The ruin inside of me was a beautiful mix of rubble that I slowly rebuilt and fortified. Happiness and success were still possible through courage when facing tough decisions and uncertain paths.

That's what being brave was, right? Choosing to face one's fears?

The pale morning sun hinted at its arrival beyond the mountains to the east, though darkness draped the road. Unfortunately, my last few weeks and repetitive sleepless nights decided they ranked higher in seniority over the coffee.

I hit the steering wheel with the butt of my hand, mostly to wake myself out of the sleepiness that weighed on my eyelids and insisted I should close them for a second. About time for a change, dammit. No more apologizing for things that weren't my fault. No more allowing others to take advantage of my situation or make excuses for mistakes I knew to be mine alone. I needed to do something about it. No one else would stick up for me.

A ripple of determination coursed through my veins as I realized I continued to live under the illusion of oppression. My freedom had been around for a while, but I continued to wear my shame for something another did to me.

My face nearly split with a yawn. After the third, my eyes watered and the road before me blurred.

In my moment of clarity, I vowed it would all end now. I would rid myself of the "battered woman" label on the walls I built around my heart and never apologize for things I didn't do again.

The podcast ended, and I turned on my favorite band. Unfortunately, one of their slow songs came on, entrancing my sleep-deprived mind. I couldn't wait to get home.

EIGHT

ORION

The time had come to leave our campsite in the park. Big Sur made camping a delight between less crowded beaches and cozy campgrounds. Thor wasn't feeling the ocean at first, but then he got into it and played in the foam while I did some short swims. Over the days and nights we stayed, he resorted to posturing himself on the beach while I swam, his head up and focused on me like a lifeguard, one who would be shit if I got into trouble. Like the guy from Into the Wild, we had to move on. Unlike Christopher McCandless, I planned for us to stay far away from Alaska and live a long time.

Thor and I were running low on food. Still plenty of water. Thor put on weight and filled in some of his excess skin. His right eye had shifted from baby blue to dusty blue, while his left eye turned a mossy green.

A thumb-nail patch of white hair had erupted on the V at the base of his neck in a lightning-like zigzag, making his name all the more fitting.

His health continued to improve. He pissed next to every redwood we passed for the first five minutes of each hike we set out on. Next to because the guy couldn't lift his leg yet. I wondered when he would. When he reached maturity? Would it be when he went through puppy adolescence? Never? I felt a bit sick over the thought he would squat forever. Surely it would be like a rite of passage. No, Thor would find the Great Balance in Dogdom. Trees and hydrants would swoon and sway with the hope of being drenched with his urine.

He totally agreed.

When I was a kid, we had a small dog that lived indoors. Rufus. A Terrier of some sort that bonded with my older brother. My grand-parents had border collies, small black and white psychos who lived to chase—cars, cattle, young boys.

Unlike those canines, Thor stuck to me like Velcro and a bit of research I did on the breed revealed their leg leaning is a consistent trait of these highly intelligent dogs. When we went for drives, he lounged in the passenger seat, back legs splayed open like a dude. With his weight gain, the position made it look like he had a little potbelly.

Maybe I should have named him Dude. Or *The Dude*.

Turned out he responded to The Dude as well as Thor.

The sun hadn't risen over the Santa Lucia Mountains; the stretch of road I drove was dark and winding as we made our way to Monterey. Brush and coastal trees reached out with skeletal fingers while resilient palm trees swayed with grace. I switched to low beams as we approached the first vehicle I had seen in miles. As I mentioned, there were curves in the road, but the driver wove between lanes like a drunkard. My phone displayed 5:48 a.m. A little too late for the drunk, or, he got an early start.

I slowed, my right arm automatically reaching down to Thor, who curled against my thigh, one paw over his nose. The vehicle, brights still blinding, swerved back into their lane and dimmed their lights. I heaved a sigh of relief and reached up to scratch my thick scruff. A hot shower and shave sounded incredible.

Thor yawned and stretched, his pink tongue curling out in a cute arc. I rubbed his head, his tags jingling, happy that little evidence of his superficial cuts and scrapes remained.

The bright headlights of a car drew my gaze back to the road and directly in front of me. I was stunned to see a woman, eyes wide with naked panic.

She frantically swerved back into her lane, but—too late—her vehicle struck the front quarter of my Bronco.

Some moments happen instantly with no room for thought. This moment stretched out like an exaggerated slow-motion movie. My Ford, clipped, spun around. Thor rolled on his back into my side, then yeeted forward when I slammed on the brakes. He yelped as he crashed into the dash.

Headlights illuminated a No Parking sign inches from the nose of the Bronco.

My ears felt stuffed with cotton. The Bronco's motor rumbled up my spine. Thor thrashed as he righted himself on the floorboard, so I threw the Bronco into park and scooped him up. His eyes were wide with fear, and he trembled in my arms.

"Hey, bud. You're okay." I hoped he was alright. He had to be.

His little booty shook with the force of his short tail wagging to show he was okay. And his tongue worked fine. He nailed my right cornea to prove it.

A panicked glance in the rear-view mirror gave me a glimpse of the other vehicle, and my heart stopped. Smoke billowed up and my taillights gave it an infernal red hue.

Fucking drunk piece of— Woman or no, she had a lot of nerve driving under the influence. "Stay, Thor." I left the truck running and slammed the door, prepared to hammer the driver with a vicious rant.

The yellow Mini Cooper, its engine still pinging, sat ghostly in the lessening darkness. Picking up my pace, I rounded the back side and circled to the front end. The driver slumped forward.

Damn it, she's hurt.

I knocked on the hood. *Bam Bam.* "Ma'am, are you alright? Miss?"

I nearly bounced off my rear bumper as I came around the car and opened her door. A warm, spicy scent rolled out with soft music. No, not soft music. Quiet blues rock.

I crouched down and gripped her shoulder, feeling firm muscles between my fingers. Struggling against the adrenaline rush, I shook her gently. "Ma'am?"

As she sat back, I noticed several things simultaneously. The gentle curve of her throat as she turned. The tiny semicolon tattoo on the inside of her wrist. Caramel and chestnut strands in her light brown hair pulled into a ponytail. A thin white tank and light gray fleece shorts on her muscular frame. A dusting of freckles across her shoulder.

"Oh." She raised a hand to her head and looked around. Her dark eyes met mine. "Oh."

"You were in an accident. Are you alright?"

"What—" She blinked slowly and took an extra second to consider if she was indeed okay. "Yes. I think so." She rubbed her forehead. "Maybe a bump. My airbag didn't deploy..." She looked around her vehicle.

"Have you been drinking?" My words came out clipped. No matter how pretty a face, drunk driving was an inexcusable offense whether or not she had damaged my vehicle.

"No."

"No?" I barked squinting at her in the dim light, the dashboard glow casting her face in a strange shadow. I had forgotten the question.

She shifted, throwing her legs out, sneakers hitting the pavement. "No. I haven't been drinking. Wish I had." She gave a rueful laugh. A dimple flashed on her left cheek. "I fell asleep. I'm so sorry." She sucked in a breath.

"Are you hurt somewhere else?"

Her lips rolled in, and she bit down on them, the dimple appearing once more. I guessed her to be five-foot-nine, a couple of inches shorter than me. Her eyes met mine, and I discovered they were a deep green. She crossed her arms, and I glanced down. The early morning was cool, and the snug tank left little to the imagination. I cleared my throat, my eyes darting back up to meet hers.

Her head careened to one side to get a look at the Bronco. "No. I'm fine. I'm very sorry about your truck."

"Hold it. You are never supposed to admit fault in an accident." I was now pissed that I couldn't be pissed at her. She told the truth. I didn't smell alcohol, and she looked gorgeous, I mean, exhausted. And familiar.

"I'm sorry. I've been working since seven-thirty yesterday." She rubbed her arms, her biceps flexing.

I swallowed as I considered her words. "Last night?" My brow dipped. Her muscles weren't like a bodybuilder or weightlifter. They were lean and defined. Showed strength.

She yawned behind her hand. "Morning. Gah. Okay. How's this go? Do we exchange insurance information? Call the cops?"

Lights from an oncoming vehicle shone in the distance.

"Let's pull onto the shoulder first."

She clicked her tongue and pointed a finger gun at me. "Grand idea." That damn dimple showed itself again as she smiled.

Too cheery for that early in the morning following a fender bender. I got in my truck, reversed, and then pulled forward, parking past the No Parking sign.

The Mini Cooper remained in the middle of the two-lane highway.

Her window rolled down as I approached, and I heard her explain her car wouldn't start. As the other vehicle bore down on us, motor screaming like a race car, I began waving my arms to get the driver's attention.

It slowed and passed by; the engine revving as the driver sped up. Ahh, the friendly West Coast. At least the driver slowed to go around.

"Throw 'er in neutral and I'll push." I pointed to the other side of the road closest to the ocean.

She nodded.

After it was safely out of the way, I invited her to my Bronco, where we could chat without her getting more chilled in the cool air. Before I climbed in, I let Thor out for a potty break.

His butt twitched in delight as he ran towards the woman, a new face to lick. I watched him stumble and fall on the road, whimpering in pain.

My vision tunneled. "Holy shit." It hit me hard and fast.

"Oh, no. He's hurt." She got to his side first and picked him up, cradling him like a baby as she rounded the Bronco to the passenger side.

It surprised me how much the puppy meant to me, and I wanted to tear him from her arms. Instead, I climbed in the driver's side, prepared to collect him.

Inside, she loved on Thor as she appeared to examine him. "Look. Again, I am so, so sorry. I'm a vet, though. I practice over in Carmel Valley and can check him out. Do rads if needed. No charge, of course, since his injuries are my fault."

It hit me that this lady was way too nice. Thor could have been limping before, for all she knew. But it was the best option. "That would be great." In and out. Get him checked. Then we would be on our way. Figure out where to get my Baja repaired. The cab of my truck felt too confined.

"Is your Bronco safe to drive?"

I mumbled something that resembled an affirmative.

No matter his pain level, Thor buckled down and achieved his main objective in life—running his tongue over her skin, specifically her cheeks and neck. A full-body flush ran through me as I realized I was suddenly jealous of that pup. I gave a curt nod, a surge of annoyance at the momentary distraction.

That's all she was. A blip in my journey to lose myself in order to find my purpose.

NINE

DANI

My insides were all over the place. What the fuck just happened? I nearly killed a man. Nearly died myself. And an adorable puppy was gluing me back together with its snuggles.

I apologized several more times while scheming to get his vehicle fixed up.

Thor finally ran out of saliva or tongue strength and cuddled up to me, curling up in my lap. He was so warm and wiggly and soft, unlike his grumpy, sharp-edged owner who had sleek, corded muscular arms. A feather tattoo peeked from his right tee sleeve. He had a chiseled jawline beneath a sexy amount of scruff, intense blue eyes beneath a strong brow, and short, dark brown hair with curls. And his scent. Manly spice, like peppery night-blooming jasmine and vanilla with a wallop of pheromones that screamed MAN. I wanted to rub my body against him like his dog to get his scent on my skin and my clothing. Ugh, I sounded like a bitch in heat. He possessed remarkable beauty. The dog, I mean. The guy was a distraction.

My body dumped too much norepinephrine and dopamine. I was giddy with lust.

Or giddy from lack of sleep.

God, I felt awful, and I wanted to giggle. I couldn't, because he would surely doubt my declaration of sobriety.

The knowledge that I *could have killed him* sunk like a stone into my chaotic brain. I could have died. Clarity struck like a bright, clear ringing bell. I didn't want to die. Previous struggles aside, death would still be inconvenient. I had too much life. Too much to live for. My high crashed, and I sniffed. When faced with my mortality, I no longer wanted out.

Alright. Fine. *Pull your head out of your ass, Dani.*

The man, Orion, said something. Gosh, even his name was hot. Orion. *Wait, what had he said?* "Hmm? Sorry, what did you say?" Fuck. How many times had I apologized? What happened to Take-Charge-Dani? Or the Bad-Ass-Bitch-Dani? The one who did not apologize unless at fault?

Oh yeah. My resolve had been crunched in the accident.

Wait. I fucking hit the guy's vehicle. My fault. I'd get an earful from Elliot when he found out about the accident. He would berate me for damaging a Baja. And my Mini. I wanted to cry. Crying would only make me look weak. No crying. Think. Fix this. Following through on my plan, I texted Elliot about my car and Orion's. I'll get Elliot to fix the man's vehicle on my dime.

I was in a car accident. Mini bruised. Hit a Bronco on PCH near home.

A quick glance at the clock reassured me my brother would most likely be up.

He replied almost immediately. *You okay?*

My eyes watered. Again. *Yes. I'll call for a tow.*

Nope. I got it. What about the other vehicle?

He's driving us back to the clinic with his injured puppy. Thanks to me, I left out. The three dots rolled, and I knew what came next. I beat him to the table by typing: *I'm safe. He's a decent guy. I'll text when I get to the clinic.*

"What's your name, doc?"

I flashed an impossibly wide grin at him. Stopped myself from saying sorry. "Dani. Call me Dani."

"That your nickname?" His forehead creases but he refrained from looking at me or in my general direction.

I lifted my shoulder and palmed my phone. So, he's a grump, protective of his puppy, and not at all interested in me. Small talk was good for reducing anxiety during a drive between two strangers. "Short for Danica."

"Dr. Danica Lavigne," his words were soft and sensual, flowing over and through me.

Get a grip. You're not a teen. "And you are Orion Windwalker?" Gah, I hated how insecure I sounded.

"Orion Indigo Windwalker, former Marine." He frowned.

"Are your parents astrologists or Rob Reiner fans by chance?" My attempt at humor felt like it slumped at my feet, but he barked out a genuine laugh, erm, cough?

He thumbed the corner of his mouth before dropping his hand to his thigh. "Something like that. Call me Rion, please." He gave me a side glance. "You look familiar."

"Can't say we've met before."

"No." Turning his attention to me for a moment, he flashed me a sinful grin.

I imagined his lips on my flesh and suddenly it was too hot, the cab having converted into an erupting volcano. Holy hell, maybe I was dying.

"You ever watch *Parks and Rec*? Rashida Jones, that's it. You look like her but with green eyes."

I laughed, sweat forming under my pits. He noticed my eye color. What the hell? Strange fluttering in my arms and legs lit me up as I internally berated myself for reading into his words. Just because I hit an utterly attractive man didn't mean we were going to hit *it*. I was completely losing it. "You aren't the first to say that. You shouldn't disrespect Ms. Jones like that." A nervous chuckle escaped, sounding more like a meep than an actual laugh. *Come on, Dani. You're a grown-ass woman, a badass bitch. Control those rabid hormones.* "Here," I pointed, directing him to a small building in a strip mall in the valley, the sun brightly illuminating the valley.

The sign over the glass door read Carmel Valley Animal Hospital. I practically fled his vehicle with Thor in my arms, the tires still rolling to a stop. My keys jingled as I opened the lock. Inside, I keyed in a code on the alarm and turned on the lights, thinking I needed another shower to remove the slip-and-slide that had established in my undies.

TEN

ORION

T hor and I made a second visit to a vet clinic within two weeks.

The clinic had a wine shop aesthetic with wood and stone details. It made me feel all warm inside. Cozy. Or maybe it was Dr. Sunshine.

I followed her to the back where she had placed Thor on an exam table. As she listened to his heart, rubbed his neck, and palpated his sore leg, her smile rarely disappearing. She seemed to truly enjoy her work. Or she just really liked dogs.

Of course, she had an excellent patient.

"He's sore on his right foreleg. I doubt anything is broken. Soft tissue injury most likely." She cocked a hip against the exam table. "I'd like to get some rads, if that's okay? Free, obviously." She draped a hot pink stethoscope around her neck. Thankfully, she had thrown a white lab coat on over herself.

Thor sat down facing her and woofed.

"Ah, the little guy thinks it's a good idea," she said, brushing a strand of her dark hair from her face. The motion drew my eyes to her collarbone and the motley, freckled contours.

I inhaled deeply, pulling in her faint scent as well as the hospital disinfectant aroma. It overpowered and sent my mind whirling. I tapped a finger against my bottom lip. "He thinks anything is a good idea if you give him attention or food."

"How long have you had him?"

I wrinkled my nose. "A couple of weeks."

"Where did you get him? I've wanted a Weimaraner since vet school." She gazed at me with intense interest as if her examination had shifted and she now pursued poking into my brain.

As I stroked Thor's sore shoulder, he nipped my hand. Although he had needle-sharp teeth, the bite was as gentle as the handshake of a lamb that can't stand the weight of its own wool. Gentle, telling me to stop touching him. No wonder the breed was called soft-mouthed. I dropped my hands to my side and clenched them. Swallowed. "I found him alongside the road."

She waved a hand and smiled. "It's fine. You don't have to tell me."

Dani, as she asked me to call her, had been quiet on the drive, typing messages on her phone. The sound of a crow's caw announced the arrival of her notifications. "Oh, good. Okay. So, I wrecked your dog, your vehicle, and your morning."

Trying not to look around, I started stroking Thor again to keep my attention focused on him. His head tilted back until his forehead touched my chest. *What a goober.* Before I could plan a cohesive sentence, she continued.

"My brother has a body shop in Monterey and just agreed to fix your Bronco. My dime."

"It was an accident," I began. Accidents were why people carried insurance.

"Yeah, but I feel responsible. Are you from around here?" She wrinkled her button straight nose, the freckles kissing.

I shook my head. Her eyes were incredible. Every time they flashed my way, I felt caught, not trapped, but captivated. More than once, we locked eyes and if our gazes could have held for eternity, it would not have been long enough. Getting lost in those eyes promised I would find myself.

Could I admit to tearing my eyes from hers first? Nope. I've no idea who broke first.

She chewed on her bottom lip. "Is it possible for you to wait for the parts? It might be a week or two."

Parts. Right. My Bronco. Vintage. Classic. I cleared my throat. Knowing my vehicle, the wait time sounded apt. I could continue my aimless wanderings around the area. Reconnect with my therapist. Saying no felt like it would disappoint Dani, and that idea made me feel strangely sad.

I nodded.

"Not one to waste words, are ya?" She grinned and gathered Thor to her, the back of her hand brushing my abdomen. "It would be best if I sedated him. Are you okay with that?"

I nodded, following her into a closet-sized room with another cool stainless-steel table. I sat in a chair and held him while she gave him an injection in a vein in his foreleg. He succumbed almost instantly. His limp form caused my insides to twist uncomfortably. Although she handled him with care, his head flopped once. Lifeless. Boneless.

And suddenly I was not in an animal sick bay. I was falling. Struggling to breathe.

"I need to use the head," I snapped.

Dani stopped arranging my sedated puppy on the table and pulled me out of the room. "Down the hall to the left."

I caught the look in her eyes. Concern. I didn't get weak at the sight of blood or medical procedures. I wanted to explain I was not a wuss. Wasn't I, though? Weak. The panic attacks. Not telling people what happened.

The disinfectant smell rose like a cloud of noxious fog before a vampire attack. Unfortunately, trying to turn it into a fantasy scene didn't lessen the flaring anxiety.

In the restroom, I turned on the faucet. Splashed cool water on my face and neck. Took a Xanax. Stared at the man in the mirror. At the pained, grizzled appearance. The wild eyes. Eyes that had witnessed too many violent, vile assignments. Had watched brothers-in-arms die in gruesome...

God damn it.

To think about one instance was to see them all at once, layered together into a merlot-colored Rorschach blot until it imprinted itself over my haggard reflection.

I blinked, and it faded.

My pulse thundered in my head, a herd of charging thoughts and images hell bent on stampeding me.

Closing my eyes, I dipped my chin, tucking it into my chest, and breathed.

Exhaled.

Inhaled.

Exhaled.

Inhaled.

My name is Orion Indigo Windwalker, and I have no fucking clue what I'm doing.

I should call home. Or be at home. With my parents. I snorted. *Thirty years old and living at home. How tragically pathetic.*

Some days, I hated the voice in my head.

I stayed inside the small restroom until I felt the Xanax kicked in, a warm, soothing calm draping over me from the inside out. My scalp tingled, but my breathing came easier.

I found Dani and Thor back in the open treatment area. She held a syringe, the needle cap in her mouth.

"Oh, good. Daddy's here."

Her words unsettled me.

"Are you alright?"

Loaded words. Was I alright? As alright as I would ever be, I supposed. Vertical and breathing. I nodded.

She injected a minuscule amount of clear liquid into the muscles of his hind leg, then sucked the spit off the plastic before capping the needle. "Sorry. Terrible habit of mine." She gestured with the capped syringe before disposing of it in the red sharps container. "We are all done. Thor will be up in a few moments. Do you mind watching him?"

I stepped up and she brushed past me and I caught a whiff of her scent, which made me simultaneously hungry and horny. Two sides of the same coin with her.

I pursed my lips, but they moved almost without my permission. "You asked before where I got him? I really found him curled up near the highway. He was pretty beat up."

"Oh?" She tapped his rabies tag. "And you got him fixed up. Vaccinated." Her eyes glistened, and she blinked. Looked away. I watched her slender neck move as she swallowed.

My stomach growled, a sound that shifted her mood.

Her sharp gaze darted between my abdomen and my mouth. "Would you like a coffee? I don't have anything to eat unless I swipe somebody's leftovers."

"Coffee would be great. Thank you, ma'am."

"Dani, please." She held up a palm, then swiveled on her heel and walked away.

Thor heaved a great sigh but remained snoozing.

"Dani." Lucky for me, she had already disappeared from the room when I uttered her name. I sounded like a jackass, or worse.

She brought two mugs back, the aroma of coffee alone giving me a buzz.

"Here is Thor's handsome skeleton." Dani pointed to a computer screen and scrolled through black and white shots of the puppy's body. Finally, she settled on one and pointed out his bones.

Thoracic vertebrae.

Dorsal border of the scapula.

Lateral epicondyle.

Radius.

Olecranon.

Carpal.

As she spoke, the words curled around me like a spell, many familiar. I don't think she uttered them to impress or show her knowledge. It was like she was ticking boxes in her head, searching for issues.

And it was hot.

"Nothing's broken, so I'll treat him for soft tissue injuries. A shot for pain relief now and some pills for a week. Since you are willing to stick around for repairs, why don't you bring Thor back for a checkup, too?"

I could hear my voice take on a sharp edge as I replied, "Only if it's free." While I didn't have a place to be, staying close to the area meant less travel and staying close to her. And that scared me.

I struggled with dealing with my own shit.

Way to get ahead of yourself, dickhead, I thought.

Her forehead wrinkled, then her face became expressionless before donning a wide, and very fake smile. "Of course. I want to make this right. Does he need any booster shots, too? I can throw those in as well."

I heaved a sigh and forced a smile onto my face. It felt foreign, like my lips were barely capable of the movement. "He does, but you don't have to. I can pay for his shots. Thank you," I said. "You did right by Thor. We'll see about my truck. And you win points with the coffee," I lifted it in a mock toast then and took a sip. "Mm. Yep. Wonderful coffee."

"Sorry, you probably should dock me points. We have one of those single serve instant coffee makers."

What was the reason for her constant apologies? "No sorries needed. It's a tasty roast and has caffeine. Good enough. Points." My smile came more easily, and she responded, her expression softening at my words.

She clapped her hands together, and Thor's head jerked at the sound. Then he yawned, his mouth gaping wide, a bit of a popping noise from his throat.

Like the roll of the ocean, Dani's yawn followed. I couldn't stop my yawn, which matched theirs, due to sudden exhaustion unrelated to Xanax.

"My brother said to bring you over when you are ready. Do you want to head there now?"

I looked at Thor, who sat on his haunches, licking his front leg. "Sure. But aren't you tired?" I often wondered about people like her. Despite being on the job for 22 hours, she's still functioning. Well, she had hit my vehicle with hers.

Being in the Marines, it wasn't abnormal to work long days and nights. We worked until we finished a mission or a task, catching a catnap when we could. Training involved sleep deprivation and missions sometimes demanded it.

Her smile drew my attention to her lips. Glossy and light pink. Perfect for kissing.

"Kidding? I insta-brewed three espresso shots into my coffee. Plus, I need a vehicle for myself. Do you mind giving me a ride to the shop?"

"Okay." The Xanax had kicked in fully. A gentle wave of relaxation rolled through me like a full-body sigh. If I'm stuck here for a while, hanging out with Dr. Sunshine might improve my mood.

ELeven

DANI

One of my clients once asked me to neuter a cat during a farm visit. A tom. The family didn't want him to leave the place or become the country's Cat Father.

The cat was one of the last things to take care of. The owner left, which was fine. I toiled away at the tomcat solo. He was just a wee youngster. His purr was anything but gentle as it rivaled a lawn mower. When I'd finished, I worked on paperwork from other tasks for the client until someone arrived. Their son had eventually and helped me catch and vaccinate the dogs. Kyle was a good kid. Smart. Working toward an Ivy League scholarship.

He offered me water before I left, so I followed him back into the garage and waited. While he disappeared into the house on his water hunt, I checked on my recovering patient who continued to sleep off the anesthesia. The surgery site looked clean. I tucked a blanket around him. One of the other young cats approached, her motor running vicariously. She kneaded the sleeping cat's back, then settled in to rest and guard.

Kyle returned with a cold water bottle and a bright, contagious grin.

"Thank you, Dr. Lavigne."

I began to tell him about the tomcat, but Kyle spotted him and bent down. He scooped up the cat, the limp body hanging from his grasp. Kyle gaped, frozen in place like an ice statue before he dropped the cat.

Dropped him!

The cat made a soft, yet melodramatic crash landing. Meanwhile, Kyle's eyes widened to the point of looking like they could actually pop out of his head, while his face remained as white as a ghost. I knew I needed to talk him through it... or find an extra-large pillow for him to collapse on.

"I neutered him," I said as I knelt and repositioned the cat. His bed buddy had stayed close by and curled back up as I checked the incision one last time. "He's sedated and will be for a while."

"Oh."

I heard Kyle's swallow.

"I thought..."

"Sorry, Kyle. I thought..."

We both spoke at the same time. I figured he knew I anesthetized the animal for surgery. I should have known better. Not everyone understands or is okay with medicine. My brother, Eamon, passes out cold at the sight of blood.

Right after Thor went limp, I noticed a subtle shift in Orion. The skin pallor. Widened eyes. The bob of his Adam's apple. His vacant expression towards Thor.

I shook Orion's shoulder to get his attention. "Eyes on me, Orion."

His blank stare filled with confusion and fear. "Where's the head?" he demanded. His voice was strained, and it had nothing to do with Thor.

When I didn't answer immediately, he went from panicked to hard-eyed. "Where's the head?" he repeated, his clipped tone signaling an underlying pain.

I shooed him away with a sassy flick of my wrist and an exaggerated twirl toward the door. His backward glance almost melted my heart and made me run after him, but I reminded myself that everyone has their own issues to face. How could I fix him when I failed daily at fixing myself?

We all have our burdens to bear.

ORION

Dani waved at someone parking in the parking lot as we climbed in my Bronco, but she only partially paid mind to the person she waved at, her focus more on her phone. "That's the receptionist, Carol." Her eyebrows furrowed as she thumbed her phone screen. "Sorry. I'm texting her I just left. So." Turning to me, she smiled, her teeth catching the corner of her bottom lip. "Where are you from?" She pulled Thor into her lap and hugged him. He groaned and nuzzled her chest.

"North Dakota."

"No kidding? My colleague who recently left is from North Dakota. She went back there. Um, Minot?" She heavily emphasized a long O sound in Dakota and grinned. "That's why I was working through last night. Had her emergency shift. A couple of colicky horses and a laceration. Most likely the full moon at work."

That spiel had a lot of information to process. "Full moon?"

"Turn right at the next light. Yeah. Full moon. Bad things occur in threes. You know." Dani made a vague gesture with her free hand. "Superstitious talk."

Okay? "How many vets are at the practice?"

"Three now. We are two vets short. I'm finishing up two weeks of ER call, which is twenty-four seven. Today is my first full day off in two weeks. Although I have paperwork I need to catch up on. Maybe a nap."

"Hopefully you get more than a day off." And a full night's sleep. I signaled and turned, the city a blur in my periphery as I focused on the road and the woman beside me. "Is that, ah, sorry, but do you always work in those kinds of clothes?"

She rubbed her bare thighs. "Ah, no. I showered at the clinic before I left. Didn't want to take my stink home." She yawned. "Shit. Sorry." She buried her face in Thor's neck. "So my brother, Elliot... He owns the body shop he started working in when he was in high school. Make sure you compliment him. He butters up like toast even though he looks like a big meanie. That's his look, ya know?"

Her voice had taken on a tone reserved for babies of any species. Thor soaked up her attention. Buttered toast, indeed.

I nodded and noticed her side-eyeing the backseat. Thankfully, I had somewhat tidied the back and set the backseat up so it didn't look like I was a total slob.

"Been on the road awhile?"

Failed. I rested my elbow on my door, letting my hand fall and catch the air. "Yeah. Few months."

"Really? Work-related travel or..."

"Or. Wanted to bum around a bit. My life took a left turn and I'm not sure what direction I need to take next."

"Oh. Well, you have an excellent travel buddy."

At her light laughter, I felt myself melt, I mean, unwind a little more. "So, how did you find Thor?"

"Curled up near my Bronco." I shared the short version of finding him. No need to share my breakdown.

"No way."

"Yes way."

"A fellow eighties kid. Am I right?"

Did she want to know my age? I scratched my chin and remembered my grizzly appearance. "Yep. You know a good barber around here?"

"I don't, but Ell will."

The body shop was an unremarkable white building on Lighthouse Road in Cannery Row, near the Aquarium in Monterey. A neon sign that read High Beam glowed in the one window between a chrome door and a white garage roll-up.

A honk sounded when we entered, one of those irritating alerts to let everyone know a customer had arrived. At least it wasn't a ding-dong sound. Although, the honk came again, and again, even after the door closed.

I stood in a small front office with a counter and a rectangular lock box on the wall behind it, hanging open with hooks for keys on the inside.

Thor began wiggling, so I set him on the floor. He immediately began sniffing around. I turned to Dani who said, "Hello pretty."

She spoke to a bright orange parrot perched on a piece of driftwood mounted on the desktop. I mistook it for a stuffed bird when I walked in, but it moved. The parrot had one foot lifted. Dani pinched its beak and gave it a gentle shake before offering her hand.

"I would like to introduce Connie. She is a Conure Parrot. I didn't name her. She came named."

Connie's beak opened, her tongue moving, and the honk sound rang again.

A soft, deep voice filled the room. "And Dani talked me into giving her a home. Why else would a self-respecting body shop have a parrot? She's very persuasive," finished a giant of a man with rich black skin and thick dreads pulled back into a ponytail. Although built like a brick shithouse, he seemed a little soft in the belly. He extended a hand. "I'm Elliot." He had the firm, calloused handshake of a man who knew hard work.

"Rion."

Dani said, "It's short for O-rion." Connie rubbed her head on Dani's cheek, and Dani nuzzled the bird back, giving it a kiss on the beak. The bird stuck out its gray tongue and made kissing noises., its sharp claws dimpled Dani's skin.

I tried not to drop my gaze to her chest. The tank top looked good on Dani. The animals around here got more action than I have had in a long time.

The parrot moved from Dani's hand to her shoulder, and worked her way, beak, claw and a few wing flaps up onto Elliot's shoulder as Dani gave her brother a hug.

"Dani California. Sis, you need to get some sleep pronto. You look like shit."

She lifted a shoulder and smiled. "Ah, shucks. You say the sweetest things." Another yawn nearly split her face open.

"Why don't you head up to the apartment? I can take you home after work."

"I need to get home and feed the livestock. I can call an Uber."

Or I can give you a ride home," I interrupted, my chest tightening at the thought of, what? Not seeing her again?

"That's alright. Ell will take one look at your vehicle and I'll be stuck waiting for hours." She rolled her eyes and grinned. "I'll see Thor in a few days. Just call me. Oh, I should give you my number first." She pulled out her phone, which she had stuck into her sports bra. "What's yours?"

I rattled it off, and my phone rang.

"There. Now you have mine. Ell, what do you think about my Mini?"

Like a gawking by-stander, I observed Dani interact with her brother as they discussed her car's damage. He might have been a year older or ten. Their easy, familiar bond made me curious about their parents, if their entire family was this close, and if she had any other siblings.

"Dani. Take one of my vehicles." Elliot had his arms crossed, a stern parental look on his face.

"Nah, I couldn't..." her eyes glinted with mischief. "Unless you're offering a bike."

Elliot sighed. "No lane splitting."

Dani squealed, startling the bird, who squawked and screeched while bobbing her almost neon orange head from her perch on the large man's shoulder. Thor gave a pointed yip and squirmed into my leg. I squatted and rubbed his head.

"Of course not, mom." Dani stepped up to her brother, a picture of opposites, and motioned with her hand.

He leaned down. Dani grabbed his face and kissed his forehead. "Your hair smells fabulous. Like a sunny California auto shop." She giggled and reached for a set of keys in the lockbox.

"Put her back for me, will ya? Some of us have work." No venom laced his words as he handed her Connie.

An aching pang hit me as images of my siblings flashed through my thoughts. I knew from recent messages they were fine and as far as they knew, my deployment in the Middle East went well.

My older brother, who retired from the Marines two years ago, worked in DC as a government contractor. Somewhere in the Western Pacific on a carrier, my sister worked on Air Force jets because her eyesight disqualified her for pilot training.

And here I stood, lifting my puppy into a football carry as Elliot handed the bird off to Dani so we could look over the damage to my Bronco. He typed some notes into his phone, asked me where I found my Bronco. "Don't see many of these gems on the road."

He was right there. But since I couldn't park it in a garage, a vehicle was a vehicle.

"Man, you could sell this thing as is for some green."

I sighed at his spot-on comment. I could sell it, but I had grown fond of it. Plus, it fit me and Thor for what we needed.

The garage door rolled up, and like a rockstar, Dani emerged from the shadowed garage depths pushing a Harley Davidson Nightster 1200. Painted in matt black, aftermarket pipes and accessories make this bike more special, but still outshined by Dani. She rested the bike on the kickstand and began pulling on a full-face helmet.

"Get a jacket and pants on, Dani!" Elliot scowled and marched into the shop. "Christ, she acts like a teenager sometimes."

Dani cocked a hip and rested it on the seat of the bike, her arms crossed. The helmet hung off her fingers by the chin strap. With her light tank and shorts, running shoes, and the ebony bike, she looked like an orgasm come to life. I swallowed and looked away. She hadn't noticed me staring, her gaze trained on the ground as she chewed on her bottom lip.

Elliot returned with a denim jacket. "Here. This is Eamon's. Return it before he notices it's gone."

"So I have at least a year."

"Yeah." Elliot huffed a laugh. "I couldn't find any pants. The guys are still looking."

"I can lend you a pair of jeans," I offered. Thor licked my neck, showing his agreement with my kindness.

Dani eyed me and I swear her gaze moved like wildfire over my lower half. "I guess, if you have a belt..."

"Or I have a pair of sweats?"

Elliot shook his head. "Jeans, please. If you don't have a belt, I'll find a tarp strap."

Her light laugh rang out. "Man, what a way to end a two-week hell run. A car accident followed by a bike ride wearing loaned, oversized jeans from a handsome stranger." She gave me a wink as I handed her the jeans and a belt I had found folded neatly in my duffel. Thank God I had a clean pair. I tried unsuccessfully to not watch as she pulled on my pants and secured the waist around her middle.

Within minutes, she had donned the denim jacket, her helmet, and kicked the bike over.

There is something magical about the low, deep throated rumble of a Harley. A simultaneous relaxing and exciting sound. Add in a beautiful woman straddling said bike, and the intoxicating combination struck me dumb. Dani revved the engine three times, dropping me further into a trance, dropped her visor, and gave a finger wave before pulling out onto the street. The deep bass dropped to a distant purr as she disappeared. I felt the loss acutely, the hum of the motor seeping out of my bones, and her mischievous smile becoming a memory.

Standing there watching unknown cars pass by, I felt like an idiot. I should have smiled more. Said something witty.

"Okay, Romeo. Let's get the damage ironed out."

Once Elliot finished his inspection, he palmed his mouth and sighed. "Dani. That girl is going to work herself to the grave. Fuck. I am so glad she is okay. And that you are okay. Thank you for not being a dick."

"Yes, sir." I didn't know what else to say.

"You a soldier?"

"Marine."

He lifted his chin, assessing me, an all-too familiar wary glint in his eye.

"I know. I look like a drifter, which I am currently. Do you have a barber to recommend? I was thinking about treating myself."

He smiled, bright white teeth. "As it so happens, I do."

THIRTEEN

DANI

Not going to lie. I got home, fed my critters, then crashed in my bed wearing those jeans of Orion's. Soft and worn in all the right places, they coaxed carnal thoughts into my head. Made me feel excited, yet safe. Too tired to do anything else, I slipped into dreamland, my mind filled with the idea of Orion in my bedroom.

Dream Orion turned to me, his features shadowed by the morning light streaming into the large open windows behind him. His gruff exterior became a shell I wanted to crack, his anger stemming from fear and loss.

"Talk to me. Tell me how to help you," I said.

Orion loomed over me. With each step he took toward me, I backed until I hit a wall.

"I have nothing to say to you, Dani."

The discomfort of those words felt like sandpaper across my heart.

"But I have so much to show you." His features materialized, and even with those words, a cock-sure smile stretched across his face.

His kiss tasted of moonlit promises, while his peppery musk filled my lungs, giving me a high that I never wanted down from. My body ached for him, so I pressed into his warm, calloused hands and felt the rough rub of his scruff skate over my sensitive flesh. He moved his hot tongue across my skin, lapping and nipping. Fingers wound into my hair and jerked my head back. He bit and pinched and slapped.

I jerked back and cried out, but Orion didn't stop or apologize.

Orion was no longer there. In his place stood him. Darius.

Abandoned and facing a sick man, I withered in his harsh stare. All the warmth that had bloomed in my belly solidified into a hard lump, weighing me down. I tried to move, but my body lacked the energy. So slow. Too slow. I choked, unable to flee as his rebar-like arms caged me.

"Dani-girl, I found you at last. I missed you. I missed all the fun we used to have."

My hands pushed between us at the sneer in his words. I beat on his chest, my heart fluttering like a sparrow locked in a hawk's sight. My fingers scraped against smooth granite. "Get. Away. From me."

He didn't. Instead, he pushed me back until I landed on a bed in an unfamiliar room. I fought against his hold like a feral animal, hating the control he had over me. Hating him. He had conditioned me to believe that my pleasure was of no value, and my body was simply an object for him to use whenever and wherever he pleased.

"Come on now, Dani-girl. This will be fun. You know you love it rough." His hands ripped away my clothes as if they were paper. "It's the only way you get aroused."

At this point, I knew nothing else existed beyond violence and depravity. If I said no, he would punish me with more than just physical pain.

He was careful. The bruises he left were in easily concealable places, hidden from public scrutiny. The secret violence we shared remained within our twisted matrimony.

I knew when he was sober, he would apologize. Cry even. Beg for forgiveness. And I believed him. Asked him to stop drinking, which he did.

Until he didn't.

And then the cycle repeated.

But now, I had zero fucks left to give him. Zero.

I landed a slap to his cheek, my palm stinging. "Rot in hell, you piece of shit."

His wide smile sent a chill through my body. "I'll rot right next to you, wifie."

Terror ripped me apart, and shame pieced me back together. My body responded while my mind fought ruthlessly. But he was stronger than me. And I knew in my gut that it was better I laid there and let him have his way. It would go faster.

So I stayed frozen, knowing that the longer he took, the more pain he would inflict. But physical pain healed with time. He teased me with his touch until I was trembling from arousal, but that wasn't enough for him.

Back when we were married and my depression and medication rendered me numb and incapable of enjoyment from sex, Darius' fury and sadism grew to shocking levels. He had returned and attempted to revisit our intimate moments. With every slap and pinch, my body and mind shut down in panic. His voice echoed with disdain for me as he barked out insults and demands.

"You can fucking cry, but you can't come?" Slap. "You whore yourself for your work." Slap. "You are my slut, and my slut alone." Slap. "Give me what I deserve."

I bucked and kicked and thrashed until something gave way, some part of me fracturing with pain that reverberated through my marrow. I fell, screamed until my throat burned as I descended into a dark abyss of exhaustion. A shadow rescued me, collected me to her breast, before dropping me on my feet.

I ran.

My heart pounded against my chest, the adrenaline coursing through my veins. My feet carried me faster and farther away, but no matter how far I got, I could still feel his presence. Smell him. His maliciousness nipped at my heels and numbed me with fear.

I navigated an uneven path; the ground tripped me up. I stumbled and ripped my clothes. Blood from scratches dripped down my body, adding to an existing trail for him to follow.

I ran, frantic and unsure of my direction, but knowing if he found me, it wouldn't be good. But then I saw it—a small cottage in the middle of nowhere.

My hope renewed, I sprinted towards it with every ounce of energy left in me. Desperate for help, I flung open the door and met Orion's intense yet kind eyes.

"Are you okay?" he asked, his voice filled with genuine concern. The kindness of his voice shattered something deep within me and tears rolled down my face as he collected me into his arms and whispered comforting words.

When he pulled back and wiped away the remnants of tears from my face, a sickening chill ran through me. Orion once more steadily transformed into my nightmare—Darius. His body distorted and grew until he towered over me like a giant.

My relief evaporated, and a hollowness consumed me. I stood frozen in place like prey, quivering in panic.

Wake up!

I woke, my body zinging with violent energy. Harsh sunlight lanced through the gaps between windows and curtains, brutal on my fatigued eyes. My raw throat stung. Bunnie meowed from the floor, but he sounded so far away.

Rolling to my side, I peered over the edge of the bed and rubbed my thumb over my first two fingers. "Come here," I said, my voice hoarse.

The sight that greeted me stole my words. Bunnie sprawled on a white carpet, his dark body like a jagged void on a starkly white rug over which a scarlet pool ebbed outward. A gaping wound in his belly exposed his intestines.

I screamed Bunnie's name over and over. He turned his black lion-like head toward me, his amber eyes dull and gray. His mouth opened, but he didn't meow or purr or cry. Instead, he spoke.

"I'm coming for you." Darius's voice cooed from my cat's mouth in a sinister, babyish voice that he used to speak to our dog.

The dog he killed after I filed for divorce.

The visions clung to me like overpowering body odor. Muscles tight, I sat up in my darkened room, stiff with a bitter taste coating my mouth. My covers twisted around me, damp with sweat. Bunnie sat atop the back of the leather chair in the corner, a sentinel watching over his domain.

It had been a terrifying nightmare. Nothing more.

Bunnie jumped off the chair and made his way onto the bed where he sat next to my legs. The regal creature lifted a lion-like paw and began licking it with his rough tongue, the flash of salmon pink a flashing contrast among the black and gray fur. As I caught his gaze, he stopped, swallowed and blinked with incredible slowness. In my mind, when my cat did this very thing, it seemed to say, "You are strong. Rise above. Be proud. Clean yourself up. Get back in the game." And, whether or not that's what he meant, that's what I did. I wiped my face, stood up, took a deep breath, and went on with my life. Sitting there would change nothing. It most definitely would not change the past. Would not bring my dog back or remove any of the tar-like stains upon my blackened heart. The only path I could follow led me forward.

First, I closed my eyes and buried my face in my hands, my body giving in to the grief that begged for release. I had worked so hard to get where I was... comfortable and confident. Ever since the unidentified phone call from Wisconsin, Darius had regained a foothold in my life, and I reverted to an anxious mess. Who could ever love what I've become?

Given that every dream of mine included a fragment of him, it seemed as if he was determined to remain in my memory. Whenever I closed my eyes, he would be there in some form or another. Leering over me, watching my every move, waiting for the opportunity to strike again.

It wasn't just dreams either; even while awake, his suffocating presence lingered in the periphery. And if he now had my phone number... my false safety net billowed like a hurricane-battered flag. There remained a slim chance the call had been from a random scammer. If I were a gambler, I would put money on Darius. He radiated brilliance on a good day and became eerily cunning when off his medication.

My paranoia matched my parents' suspicions, and we took no chances.

Be rational, Dani, I thought to myself. With everything going on, it's no wonder my dreams tripped up and introduced him to my safe place. Had I ever really been safe from him in my dreams, though? Safe physically, but not mentally or emotionally. He could still wreak havoc on me.

I hated him, and that hate bled into my subconscious as it conjured up pieces of the atrocious things he had done, warping and blending with my reality.

I had thought I had forgiven him. Forgiven myself. It's necessary to move on. But forgiveness is not so easy when the injuries continued to inflame.

Fourteen

ORION

My lackluster effort to uncover more about Dani from her tight-lipped brother proved unsuccessful. Totally understood. I wouldn't give up info on my sister to some creep off the street. Besides, I would see her soon.

Ever since my discharge, I've felt awkward, out of place, like a stranger, which I was. Things were different in the Corp. Rigid structure. Familiar faces. Life had other plans, so I needed to move on.

Thor and I left and headed to a beach up the coast. As we walked along the ocean, we came upon a man, ass in the sand between two surfboards. The top portion of his wetsuit peeled off him like a half-exposed banana. When he noticed our approach, he threw a shaka.

"How are the waves?" I asked, hoping I didn't sound like a moron. I didn't know the proper terminology for surfing.

"Ankle slappers, bro. Cute puppy. What's his name?" The man had a tanned, weathered face from spending a lot of time in the California sun.

His eyes seemed permanently crinkled at the corners, weathered by sun, sea, and wind. His dark hair stuck straight in wild directions.

"Thor."

Thor approached, nose testing the air, unsure of the stranger.

"Hey, buddy. Come here," the man coaxed in a low, soft voice as he rolled to his knees.

That was all it took for Thor to warm up to the man. As he petted my puppy, I turned my gaze to the water. A line of surfers bobbed offshore.

"You surf?" he asked.

I settled on the sand next to him, taking my shoes and socks off. "No. Always wanted to learn, though."

"Ah, man. It's awesome. You from around here?"

We chatted about little things and at the end of a ten-minute conversation, I had a plan to meet him, Cage Bardell, later that afternoon for lessons. His wife, Caren with a C, who was out on the water with a new board, could babysit Thor. I had free use of his board so long as I found a wetsuit, his wife could get her puppy fix, and he could get back in the water. A major win-win for all of us. I mean, what other options did I have while I waited for repairs?

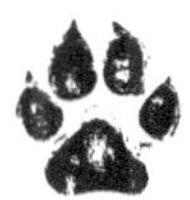

I woke at 5:45 a.m. to someone rapping on a window of the Bronco, pleasantly sore from the last four days of surfing. As I sat up, I realized some stiffness originated from whatever I had been dreaming about. My guess would be Dani, as I couldn't seem to get her out of my mind like some obsessive freak. Everywhere I had looked the past few days, I had hoped to glimpse her. Ridiculous, I know. Small-town Cali and small-town in North Dakota were worlds apart and my chances were low.

Speak of the devil and she appeared, knocking on my Bronco. She stood outside, her hands cupped around her eyes as she peered in the back window of the Bronco. My pulse spiked erratically as I held a hand up and crawled out the passenger side, pulling on a shirt as I stepped out and closed the door behind me. Thor reared up on the window so he could watch the action.

"Hey. I didn't realize you were sleeping in your Bronco," she began, her breathless tone revitalizing the tingling in my groin.

"What are you doing here?" I allowed my embarrassment to ease my arousal. Unfortunately, I also sounded like a dick. I clasped my hands and dropped them in front of me.

"Oh, sorry." Her smile faltered for a moment before reappearing. She looked away.

Dani wore a tank and shorts again, hot pink and black this time, with the same running shoes. A layer of sweat coated her flushed skin, and I noticed her earbuds.

"I live nearby and was out for a run. Saw your vehicle." She flexed her hands, the muscles rippling in her forearms. "Sorry. I didn't mean to bother you."

As she backed up, I rubbed my face. "You didn't bother me. I should be out running, but I decided to sleep in one morning."

She gave a wry chuckle. "And I interrupted it. I am very sorry."

"You've said sorry four times." I waved a hand. "Don't be. I am sorry. I don't wake up well. My sister calls me a cranky-ass bear."

Dani smiled, her look caught between embarrassed and excited, and scratched the side of her nose. "Apt description." She held up three fingers and ticked them off. "Cranky. Ass. Bear. Although the recent hedge clipping makes you less bearish."

I deserved those monikers, which riled me even as I searched for a way to erase them.

"So, you're living out of your Bronco?"

I crossed my arms, all at once self-conscious. "Yeah. That a problem?"

She shrugged and looked down. Kicked a pebble.

"I thought living in a Bronco by the ocean was a step above living in a van by the river."

Her quick laugh suggested she got the joke. "Whatcha been up to?" She drew an imaginary circle in the air between us. "Besides the shave and haircut. I damn near thought I knocked on the wrong Bronco, but the license plate matched and Thor was a dead giveaway." She laughed, my behavior failing to bother her much.

I never understood people whose smiles came so easily. Then again, people rarely understood my grim outlook on life, so there you go. I leaned back, the cool metal of the door cooling my skin through my clothing. "I've been learning how to surf."

"No shit? Guess the surfboard on the roof should have given me a clue." I nodded.

"I'd say that's why you're so salty," she winked, "but I think that's your normal, adorable personality."

Her gentle tease coaxed a smile from me.

"You said you should be running. Do you take Thor with you?" she asked.

I ran a hand through my short hair, thankful for the crewcut. No messy hair from sleep. "Usually. It's too hot to leave him alone in the vehicle." Although November along the central coast offered cooler weather, better safe than sorry.

She checked her watch. "Do you want to run with me? I have a few miles left before I turn and head home to get ready for work."

I agreed, eager to have a running partner besides Thor. He got heavy, but the guy couldn't keep up yet. And really, the prospect of spending time with Dani proved far more appealing than my imagination.

I clipped a leash to Thor just in case he needed to be on the ground, and he jumped into my arms. After I locked the Bronco, Dani greeted my pup as I held him. He wriggled in my arms and licked her face as she rubbed noses with him, cooing and giggling. Her closeness bathed me in a pleasurable warmth. Even my mouth watered as I closed my eyes to focus on the intensifying sensations. It had been a long time since I'd been in an intimate relationship, and I had no plans of entering one, but shit... the green-eyed monster reared up and wanted to butt in and replace Thor. I shook my head and laughed.

As she continued to love on my puppy, her scent wrapped around me like a hug of caramel apples, coconut, and cookies. The day couldn't have started out better. My stomach clenched and my pants became disconcertingly tight. Quite a hard thing, pun intended, to achieve in boxers and sweats.

"Are we running or petting?" I met her wide eyes, fully embracing the flirty tone.

Dani rewarded me with a pretty pink blush. "I'm done petting. For now."

I wanted to seize her face in my hands and explore her mouth, replacing her cheeky grin with lips parting in ecstasy.

Later. Maybe. It took every ounce of self-preservation I had to remind myself this place was a blip. A pin on my map.

We started off at a slow jog. "You live close?" I asked, wondering how long a run she might have already gotten in.

"Yes. Not too far from here."

Vague is as vague does. All the better. Running with someone can be healthier than running alone. A bit of competition goes a long way. Dani looked like a runner but looks could be deceiving. We chatted very little, our pace making idle chatter difficult. Her path led us off into a park where we ran side-by-side. When the way narrowed, either she or I took the lead. I football carried Thor, switching him to the other arm to even out the arm work.

I had forgotten how intimate running with someone could be. She and I spoke with body language, asking and answering. The synchronized motions, sweating, and breathing, had my mind veering into other ideas of other intensive forms of exercise. I had to adjust often in order to keep my dick from flopping around too much.

On a rise overlooking the ocean, she stopped. The sun's rays clipped the mountain behind us. Below, a glass-like ocean bloomed out to the horizon. When she looked at me and smiled, it eclipsed the sunrise.

Arriving back at my Bronco, she paused, arms crossed overhead, as she caught her breath.

"You wanna bring Thor by today?"

I nodded and set him in the back of my vehicle so I could search for a couple of water bottles. She took one and drank half. Water dribbled down her chin and splashed on the fabric stretched tight between her breasts. I caught her peering into the dim interior of my vehicle. Thor dribbled water on my calf when he sat at my shoe and leaned into me, his tiny body only adding to my own body heat.

"Good. I only work until noon. Catch ya later."

She ran off before I had the sense to plan a response, and I had never felt more alone, which spoke volumes considering loneliness and I were bosom buddies.

FIFTEEN

DANI

Could the man look hotter? I had never understood the lure of gray sweatpants on a guy until that morning. Be still my heart and shit. The guy made my mouth water. He wore the shit out of those sweatpants. Would it be weird if I said I wanted to be that pair of sweatpants? Yeah, probably. It took every ounce of control to not let me catch me staring, although I ran behind him as much as I could.

I kicked up my pace towards home and told myself to knock it off. The rando burst of horniness needed to settle. At thirty-two years of age, I had plenty of time, should have plenty of time, to find someone to rock my socks off. Although after all I've been through, the idea of being with another man troubled me. Best I stick to the B.O.B.s, or battery operated boytoys.

On the other hand, perhaps a drifter would be perfect. No strings. By the way my body buzzed when he was near suggested we had a connection, whether it was an open or closed circuit was hard to say. Well, not that hard when he appeared in his glorious sweats.

I paused in my cool down stretches to wipe away the sweat on my face with the back of my hand. My fingers fell across my heated skin, soft like butterfly kisses, and I allowed myself a few brief moments to become lost in the sensation.

To the bigger picture, I reminded myself; I messed up whatever plans he had. Besides treating Thor and getting his Bronco fixed up, I could do more to make my wrongs right.

The personal belongings cluttering his vehicle made it obvious that he was living in it. Any normal person would enjoy a hot shower, a soft bed, easy access to the laundry, right? I could offer such an option, but would he see it as pity or a handout?

The ocean-side cottage came into view as I walked through my backyard. An adorable A-frame decked out as an artist's retreat, it now stood empty, begging for relief. Relief from loneliness. Sadness. Silence.

The cottage, not me.

What I thought I knew of Orion thus far—he was proud, strong, resilient, even if he didn't accept it. He carried his demons in his pockets, but his love for Thor blazed like the sun.

I recognized something of myself in him. A loner who, at his center, was lonely. I could help. At the very least, I could offer shelter. Maybe be a distraction?

I sure as fuck needed one.

My attention turned to my phone gripped in my hand like a dead weight. No abnormal phone calls since the number change. The PI my parents hired had turned up nothing new. Darius still lived in our old home. No changes, no travels, no unusual friends. Nothing of interest in his internet search history. The Wisconsin number was a burner, a dead end.

With renewed vulnerability and feeling like my past tainted my life, I'll be the first to admit an easy distraction would be good for me. Fantastic, even.

An excitement built in me the more I thought about it. I hadn't been with anyone but my ex. Lame, I know. We met young. In the beginning, it was great. Then my acceptance into vet school disrupted our time. I graduated, got a job. Perpetual exhaustion became the mistress my husband grew jealous of.

"Give me your phone." His daily demands meant he went through my emails, calls, and messages. When social media began, he stalked everyone I followed. I ended up canceling all my accounts to avoid that drama.

Sex became a chore. One more thing to put on a to-do list. Even when the doctors put me on strict rest following a procedure.

"Come on, Dani. Your hands and your mouth still work."

I blamed my anti-depressant medication for the inability to control my mouth. "Your hands don't seem to be broken, either. Give yourself a hand job."

He hit me for the first time that night. It was the start of the end.

sixteen

ORION

As I pulled up to the Carmel Valley animal clinic, I parked next to a white Toyota truck with a slide-in veterinary box. A woman with hair in a dark braid down her back and wearing green coveralls and a gray Henley rummaged in the back. Restocking. Reorganizing? Making a mess, to be truthful.

She stood, turned, and waved. Her smile sucked the breath from my chest.

Dani.

I had seen her mere hours ago, yet my heart rate jumped at seeing her. She deserved more than being called pretty, and beautiful didn't quite cut it. Beautiful fit her heart, her kindness, her spirit. What she looked like... how it felt to be near her... Let me put it this way. Ever stand next to a wildfire? The thundering roar and devastating heat mesmerize, not from danger, but from the dance of colors and light. I knew with certainty it would be dangerous to get too close to her. Like fire, getting too close would leave me burned, and as gorgeous of a ride it would be, a certain clarity rang true. There would be no coming back from the destruction Dani would cause. And I craved her all the more for it.

My phone rang, drawing my attention. "Hello?"

"Hey, Orion. I found parts to fix your Baja. But," Elliot began.

"There is always a but," I said, bracing myself for the fallout.

"Yeah, man. I'll need at least three days to throw it all together."

The turnaround exceeded my expectations, but stuck me here for five more days with the weekend coming up. I climbed out, my phone to my ear as I talked to him. Dani strolled up, hands in her front pockets. A gold embroidered caduceus on the front right breast pocket of her bibs. Instead of running shoes, shiny brown boots stuck out beneath her hem.

Thor clambered onto the driver's side, whining behind me.

Dani gasped and said, "There's my good boy. Come here." She wedged herself between me and the Bronco door, claiming my pup through the open window. She caught my eye, winked, and stepped back.

Her coconut-apple-cookie scent blended with the earthy aroma of horse, creating a unique and exhilarating aroma.

On the phone, I said to Elliot even as my eyes stuck on Dani, "Could you fit me in next Monday instead? I need to find a place to stay while I don't have wheels."

Dani waved a hand at me while Thor chewed on her braid. "You could crash at my place," she offered in a loud whisper.

My brow dipped, and I cupped my hand over the phone speaker. "You'd put up a stranger in your home?"

She squinted her eyes and huffed a laugh. "No. I have a cottage that I rent out. It's vacant right now. No charge," she sang as she removed her hair from Thor's mouth.

Not one to stay miffed, the dog struck with his tongue, landing a solid tongue punch to her ear. "Ah, Thor. You silly beast."

Her giggle twisted me up something fierce.

I considered. Being close to her for a few days would be excellent, but I refused to take handouts. I told Elliot I'd drop by later, then hung up.

"You're going to come stay with me," Dani bounced on her toes, grinning like a little kid.

"Look. I'd be happy to take you up on your offer." I held up my palms. "But only if I pay."

She opened her mouth to protest, and I placed a finger over her lips. Her warm breath against my finger momentarily unbalancing me. But then

Thor struck again, his tongue dragging over my wrist and breaking the moment.

"Shh." I cleared my throat, removed my finger, and grabbed Thor's snout, giving it a playful little shake. "Seriously? I'm not a complete bum."

She squinted an eye at me. "You sure?"

I licked my lips and saw her gaze dart to my mouth. "Come on, Doc. Don't you have a patient to check out?" I grinned and followed her into the clinic, explaining Thor hadn't been limping for the last two days. A good turn of events.

The motion in the clinic had a similar feeling to the one Thor and I first visited. Busy. Friendly and lively with all the traffic of animals and owners.

He took his booster shot like a dog food motivated would—without notice. I held a treat in my fist, which he licked at while Dani stuck him under the loose skin behind his neck. The little dude didn't even flinch.

"Such a good patient," she said with a wink. "Alright, Orion. Let me show you to your potential short-term home."

I followed her vet truck out of town and back into Monterey, where we dropped my Bronco at Elliot's body shop. Then she drove south along the coast. Eventually, she turned right, down a private gravel road with a metal guard gate. Pine, live oak, and a willow tree hide the lot from view of the highway. Box-shaped ficus hedges lined the driveway, the ground tidy with pebble landscaping.

A two-story Craftsman house appeared from behind the hedgerows. With a traditional wraparound porch and exposed wood beams, the place was both sublime and cozy. It had green, gray, and blue-colored stone siding, while the roof shingles pulled in browns to match the beams.

Cozy and massive.

I knew a few veterinarians in my childhood and none of them made enough to cover a mortgage like this.

Then again, this was California. Who knew what her story was?

Dani California.

Dani was neither superficial nor plastic, like the Red Hot Chili Peppers song. And like the clarity from earlier, I knew without doubt I would mourn the day she no longer had a spot in my life.

She parked in front of a detached two-car garage, hopped out, and flagged me. Thor and I followed, happy to stretch our legs. Down the driveway, right next to a rocky rise overlooking the Pacific, stood a tiny fairytale-esque cottage. Crazily cut cedar shingles covered a rolling, tall, asymmetrical roof. Yellow sandstone decorated the portico.

"This is the place you rent out?" I asked. "Who were the last renters? Hansel and Gretel?"

"Ha. No. It's cute, though, right? Or too cute for you?"

"I don't know," I joked. Or tried to. I scratched my neck, and I wondered if I should let the beard grow again. Maybe it was too cute for me. I'd feel more comfortable as the Big Bad Wolf.

"Well, the price is right. Right?"

"You haven't told me the price," I reminded. "I have asked, but you just duck the question."

She opened the front door with a key and waved me in. "I forgot."

Inside was a large open room with a blend of ivory, light greens, and pale grays with a smattering of orange and teal accents. Dani set two reusable grocery totes that held Thor's dishes, food, and toys, along with a bit of my food on the counter. A full kitchen with seating along the peninsula greeted me upon entry, with a floor-to-ceiling fireplace at the opposite end.

She gave me a tour. "Here is the bathroom. Sorry. Only a shower."

"Better than my Bronco."

"You seem to do fine. Still smell yummy." Her cheeks turned an adorable shade of pink and she looked away.

The upstairs exposed A-frame roof held a bed and dresser, a railing opened the room to the floor before.

"What do you think? Too cute for you to stay in a few days?"

She stood beside me at the top of the stairs while Thor attempted to climb the smooth wood up to us. Even with the hint of horse, she smelled incredible.

A beep sounded.

The excitement drained from her face. "Sorry. My alarm. I have a house call this afternoon. Couple of horses. You good?" She slapped her fist against her thigh.

I dropped my backpack and duffle on the floor. "Yep. I'm good. You sure you don't need to throw on a cape or something?"

She pressed her lips together, trying to conceal a smile. "No cape. That's for bullfighting and superheroes. I'm just going to grind down a couple of old horses' teeth so they can eat."

"Sounds like a job not many can do." I crossed my arms. "Superhero."

Her eyes darted between my arms and my chest. I tried not to flex too much.

"Whatever. Behind the house, there's a trail to the ocean. If you see a young girl around, don't scare her off, please. She's my neighbor's kid who stops in to help me out."

Before I could ask *what* she meant, Dani trounced down the stairs to the ground floor, giving Thor a quick pet as she went by.

seventeen

ORION

After scoping out the cottage, Thor and I ventured outside. A cool, stiff breeze from the sea buffeted us as we made our way down the rock and scrub-lined path to a small patch of sand. Rocky cliffs surrounding the area and added to the sense of seclusion.

We stayed out until sunset. I fell asleep on a beach towel I brought from the cottage. When I woke, Thor snoozed, cuddled into my side. The breeze had shifted and felt warmth upon my face.

When we returned to the yard, Thor sniffed around the display of irregularly shaped paving stones in front of the cottage. Tufts of spindly grass poked up here and there. He tasted a few for good measure. Decided they were better used as a toilet.

Lights were on at the big house, and I wondered what she was doing. Not that I didn't wonder that a lot. A bird screeched in the nearby trees, startling Thor. Instead of running to my leg, he stilled and, nose in the air, lifted a front leg.

"Come on, bud. The bird sounds bigger than you."

Thor huffed his disagreement but followed me inside. I looked around the spotless, bare kitchen and considered my options. No food to prepare for dinner. Call for delivery? I didn't know the address, although I could find it in my phone app. Go without? My stomach reminded me we hadn't had lunch.

Instead of deciding, I took a shower.

While the water heated, I set a bowl of food and water in the bathroom for Thor. I left the door open a crack, since the bathroom lacked a fan. I doubted the pup would wander, especially with the fluffy rug to curl up on.

Steam moderately hazed the top of the shower stall, but I could keep an eye easily enough on Thor. I stepped beneath the hot water and fell into a meditative breathing pattern as Satan's tongue licked my spine. With each inhale and exhale, I focused on the flow of air until my thoughts backed into a corner, quiet and out of sight.

I gazed unfocused at the white tile floor where the water pooled and drained away. I liked to imagine the water catching my worries and carrying them down the drain. Instead, the white reminded me of Dani's white tank top. Like any other obsessive moment, an image of Dani triggered a rush of scenarios. What I might say for her to favor me with a smile. A laugh. A look.

A hunger built within me unrelated to food. Wild and urgent. The streams of water coursing down my body became her hands, her mouth, her tongue.

I washed, soaping my hands and starting with my hair and face. In the bright white stall, I closed my eyes and pictured Dani. A spectral version of her moved through my thoughts.

Early in my treatment, my medications numbed me to the point I couldn't feel anything. Detached. Emotionless. Life became monochromatic and dull.

Then came my discharge and change in meds. Feelings came back. Since meeting Thor, I've experienced a refreshing sense of awakening.

Since meeting Dani... it felt like I walked inside a kaleidoscope. My steps were lighter. The barbed wire around my chest had disappeared. I'm not sure when the loss occurred, whether gradual or sudden, but I didn't recognize it until then. I relished in that lightness and color that radiated from her.

I rinsed and braced my forearm on the wall below the showerhead, leaning forward. My other hand found my swollen cock, a problem that seemed to arise frequently since meeting Dani as if reverted to my teen self. A scent or bit of friction or the mere image of her face would set me off, hard and antsy.

Dani's hands would look much better. What would happen if I allowed myself to drop my guard with her? Would she be interested in something physical? I had no plans to stay around. Was it worth using her body while here?

I flexed and strained into my grip until my climax slammed into me, leaving me breathless but still wanting. I knew without a doubt a taste of her wouldn't be enough.

Suddenly, exhaustion slammed into me with the realization of my pathetic state. Empty, sad, and lonely. Depression was fucking depressing.

A noise startled me. I peered through the clear shower stall side. No Thor to be found, and the door stood wide open. The steam had dissipated from the small room. The last thing I needed was for him to chew the shit out of something.

Shutting the water off, I called for him, but heard nothing. I palm-scraped the water from myself a bit and realized I didn't have a towel. Recalling Dani pointing out that the closet out in the hall next to the bathroom held linens, I called to Thor again as I stepped out of the bathroom, into the hall.

I opened a closet door and found a towel on the middle shelf, between toilet paper and cleaning supplies below, and bed linens and extra pillows above. I closed the door, wiped my face, then heard noises in the kitchen.

"Thor?" I called.

"And me," replied a sing-song voice. Dani walked into view and stood at the end of the kitchen peninsula. She paused, mouth open and eyes wide, before glancing away.

I lowered the towel to cover the area below my waist.

"Hi. Sorry." She sounded winded, and her face flushed red.

I stood there like an idiot as Thor rushed over and began licking the water running down my legs.

I wondered if she opened the door to the bathroom.

Naw. Why would she do that?

"Sorry for what?"

"Interrupting." She rolled her lips inward and bit down, one cute dimple displaying.

"I was just thinking about you." I gave her a cocky smile and waited to see if her reaction would reveal if she had witnessed more than my naked lower half, then chided myself over being foolish. Better not to flirt with her.

She glanced at me, then looked away and coughed. "I forgot to ask you about dinner earlier, so I texted you but hadn't heard and since you don't have a vehicle, I thought I could invite you over, but it's Wednesday."

I raised my eyebrows and wrapped the towel around my waist as I walked into the light from the kitchen. Wednesday? What was the connection? And why the rambling?

"Right." She licked her lips as she walked into the kitchen, placing the peninsular between us. "Wednesday is girls' night. I have a few friends over and we sit in the hot tub."

"And your regular male stripper canceled, so you are looking for a new one?"

Her head nearly twisted off her head as she looked back at me. "What?"

"What?" I placed my hands wide apart on top of the counter and leaned forward. She had yet to give me vibes that she wasn't interested in me. With my recent masturbation sess finished, I was relaxed, yet still horny.

It didn't help thinking she might have spied on me. The idea of her watching made me harder. Also, I could see she wore a bikini beneath her tank top. And she added fuel to my imagination with her comment about a hot tub.

Dani gave me a crooked smile. She walked to the counter across from me and mirrored my position. "Why, Orion, are you offering to dance nude for me and my friends?"

I gave her a lazy, panty-dropping grin. "Only if you uninvite your friends."

Her delicate eyebrows rose. "Hmm. It's not much of a strip tease when you're only wearing a towel." She leaned across the barrier between us. "And I've already seen your junk."

"Oh, and not to your liking? I retract my offer." Some emotion flashed across her face. Regret? "Fine. Don't call off your visitors."

Genuine disappointment read like a neon sign.

Was she flirting? Was I? I was so out of practice. Did it matter? No. I had enough baggage overflowing with shit and I shouldn't dump it here. Besides, that baggage included a clueless family back home that I had to face eventually.

Then again, a little extraneous activity with this beauty could be fun. No harm in that, right? "Stay here for a bit and let them have their fun without you."

"Why would I do that?" She arched an eyebrow.

My skin tingled as her eyes drank me in. "So I can learn how your body feels against mine."

We both flinched as someone yelled her name from outside.

She whispered, "You're trouble, Orion."

"Glad to hear it, Dani."

Thor walked up and scratched at my mutilated lower limb with his paw. My scarred calf muscles twitched, and it took all my effort to withhold my attention from the misshapen area. Unfortunately, flashes of the incident that led to my injury fluttered at my consciousness and siphoned off my happy vibe. Thor plopped his bony ass on my bare foot and leaned into me. I beat down the urge to push him away, but couldn't help the wince that passed over my expression.

She scratched her nose and stepped back. Tugged her tank away from her chest. A silver chain glinted at her throat. "I should go. But I brought you some lasagna, beer, milk, coffee, and a few other groceries. Call me if you need any sugar." She looked down at her hands with a small smile. "And you are welcome to stay longer. I have a renter starting next month, so that gives you a couple of weeks to bum around, have a home base, surf all you want. Oh, and I talked to Elliot. He has a loner car you can use. Or the bike. Do you ride motorcycles?"

It was as if her kind words finished sucking all my energy and purpose out of me, and suddenly I struggled to take in a ragged breath. What exactly triggered me? Something she said? Or had it started before with Thor? I didn't allow myself to dive in and determine. Instead, I reacted. "You can't fix me with your handouts or your charity," I spat.

Her body stiffened, tension bleeding into her. Voice quiet, she gave an eerily calm smile, belying her stiff posture. "What's there to fix? I am offering help. It's not charity, Orion. I know—"

"You know nothing about me. I could be a serial killer or a rapist for all you know. You don't know me."

She exhaled slowly, and her voice lowered, calm and easy. "You're right. I don't know you. What you've been through. How you feel. And even if you told me, there's no way I could fully understand. I am only offering friendship. Sorry, I'll go."

Fuck. Why was she always apologizing? Oh wait, I had transformed into Mr. Asshat. Her abrupt face struck me as odd. My anger got the best of me and instead of replying in anger, she spoke to me like I was a snarling, rabid dog.

God, I was such a dick.

"Look, Dani." I stepped sideways, wanting to get around the peninsula between us, but she stepped back. I wondered if I killed any chance of her wanting to get to know me in the future.

She held up her palms. "It's okay. I'll leave you alone."

Then she left, leaving me to wallow in a good heap of self-loathing.

EIGHTEEN

DANI

W as he this attentive to all women? And the way he spoke to me was direct and refreshing. No beating around the bush with him. Even so, my insecurities were in overdrive, as was my need for reassurance. Fucking insecurities.

Shit. Shit. Shitty-shit. I questioned my judgment. After that exchange, I lusted after him, even though he set off multiple alarms.

What the fuck had I seen?

My swimsuit stuck in all the wrong places as I made my way back to the main house. My guests were waiting, but all I wanted to do was head back and demand either: A) what the fuck his problem was, or B) he put his tool to better use. He had offered, hadn't he? Or had I imagined it?

Holy Hannah, he was gorgeous.

"Dani, you okay? You look pale."

"Just thirsty," I said to Camile, Eamon's wife, my gorgeous sister-in-law and mother of my niece. Thirsty for a strong gulp of Orion.

Unlike my mom, who wore her sleek black hair in a pixie cut with side-swept bangs, Camile's hair piled on top of her head in a loose bun. Stray locks hung around her face. Camile had the same brown skin with cool, jewel undertones like Elliot and our mother. Her easy charisma made everyone fall in love with her.

My brothers and I were close, but their wives and I were closer thanks to the monthly gatherings at my ocean-side abode. My parents actually owned it but had put the offer on the table for me to buy it. I couldn't have said yes faster. We only needed to take the time to draw up paperwork.

"Here you go, baby girl." Camile handed me a glass of red wine.

I took a deep drink. Ah, the good stuff. The ultra smooth, sweet red berries and peppery spices of my favorite Australian Shiraz filled my mouth and set off a cascade of delicious shivers in my body. I sighed and tipped my glass toward my mother. "Love your new hairstyle, Mom."

She patted her head, the pixie cut with side-swept bangs giving her a youthful appearance. Mom smiled shyly. "Your father is struggling with it. Makes him feel like he's living with another woman. Best way to spice things up in the bedroom, though."

My company hooted and cheered at my mother's slightly disturbing comment. The short hair differed dramatically from her wavy black tresses that once hung down to the middle of her back.

"Dani," my mom gestured with her wineglass toward the house. "Have you turned off the back camera?"

Mom, ever cautious, preferred our girls' nights to be uncensored or videoed, hence the question. No doubt it was in her mind, too, that maybe having it off wasn't the brightest idea, but we needed a night to unwind. Besides, no way Darius could encroach on our small Cali town without the PI's notice.

"We are a go, ladies. Keep your bathing suits on, please. I do have someone staying in the cottage."

"Who is it this time, baby girl?" Camile threw her arm around my shoulder as I eased into the hot tub. Her hair weighed down by the steam, clung to her neck.

The water soothed my aches. "Some guy I ran into." No truer words had ever been uttered in the history of Danica Lavigne. My smirk echoed the odd feelings bubbling in my interior.

A gasp followed by, "The Marine?" Ginger, Elliot's wife, asked. "Elly says he's trouble, Dani."

That's an understatement. "Because he's hot?" I asked without thinking. Of course, Elliot would think any man I might have an iota of interest in was trouble. Understatement of the century, and not because of my ex, but because he was the type of older brother to weed through any potential partner with a fine-tooth comb.

Mom chimed in, "Pull him up."

I sighed, dropping my head against Camile's arm. Once they saw him, there would be no going back. I grabbed my phone, and with Camile resting her chin on my shoulder while I searched, her curls stuck to my cheek as we scanned through security pictures. I felt like a stalker.

"That's who's in the cottage? Right now? Alone?" Ginger's younger sister, Dawson, asked when I flashed my selected photo. "Why is he alone? What's wrong with him?"

The picture showed him shirtless with Thor as they walked up from the beach that afternoon. Lucky for Orion, I didn't have cameras inside the cottage. His bronzed chest seemed to glow from within. Add in the curves of his muscles, the ridge below his abs that dipped down beneath the waistband of his shorts, and my mouth watered. I couldn't make out the tattoo on his left upper arm, but the right side looked like a dream catcher.

"And you're up here with us? What is wrong with you?" Dawson asked. "Is he gay?"

I bit down on my lips and squinted one eye while I thought about it. "I don't think so." His offer might have been a joke, though.

Ginger shook her head. "Nope. He is not. He has the hots for Dani."

The heat from the hot tub had me sweating already. "Definitely not."

"Me thinks Dani-darling protests too much." Dawson was a literature geek and high school English teacher in Monterey.

"Me thinks I would enjoy a bedroom rodeo with the stallion if he was so inclined. Alas, he rides alone." I squirmed at the scene I'd witnessed earlier when I peeked into the bathroom to see why it hung open. Of course, I heard the shower running. And wet movements and low grunts and moans. The steam limited my view of his toned backside, but his movements left little to my imagination. I had allowed myself a few moments of ogling... I mean admiration, struck by the power that coiled within his body. My body reached overheating levels as I recalled his words, "So I can learn how your body feels against mine."

Had he really wanted me, or did he flirt like that with every woman he meets?

The sight of him holding his towel while water dropped and ran from every sensual dip and curve of his masculinity struck an aching inside that needed attention at some point. I stopped myself from picturing his body moving over mine. There were ladies present, and I was already one step away from racing back to the cottage.

Good God, the power radiating off him could turn heads for miles. But did he find me attractive, too? I mean, his nether region reaction suggested he might, but it wasn't an absolute stamp of approval. It could have been the cool kiss of the evening air that felt good to him.

"I think you need to text him right now. Foxtrot Uniform Charlie Kilo Mike Echo."

It took me a minute to decipher what Ginger said. "Ahh, good one. Use military lingo. Because he's a Marine." I rolled my eyes. "He's not interested."

"He's a former Marine. Discharged for medical reasons," my mom chimed in. Of course, she had already run an extensive background check.

"You going to share anything else?" I raised an eyebrow.

"I'll email what I found to you. He seems decent enough. Never married. Driven, but his military career cut short following a major incident in Syria."

Having seen his calf, I knew he had been physically injured. I gathered there were plenty of mental wounds buried deeply. Unseen damage he struggled with. Not unlike me. Two people hooking up with overflowing emotional baggage does not make for a reduced amount of said emotional baggage.

"Baby, don't let life pass you by without taking chances. We are here for you," she and my sisters-of-my-heart raised their glasses, "and beg to live vicariously through your wild tales. Because, you know, we're off the market."

At my snort, Mom added with a laugh, "All right, fewer details for me."

Ginger spoke again. "But seriously, if you want to ride this wild stallion, then ask."

"Ask? Like, point blank? Do you wanna go for a ride?" Really? Here I thought one had to flirt and fawn and cook to catch a guy. Was that the way to go nowadays? I mean, he blatantly offered. Kinda. But still. He could have been joking.

"No. Forward works well. No mixed signals." Camille offered. "That's how I roped Eamon into falling for me." She waved a hand near her throat.

"Right. It had nothing to do with... all that." I moved my hand in a big circle.

Camille giggled.

I let their bright laughter wash over me, pulling away the ugly doubts the more I submerged myself in their presence. Being with my family, the girls, lifted my spirits. Plenty of chatter about family matters, inappropriate jokes, wine, and my present worries spent time in the shadows for the first time in a long while. They stayed the night as always, preventing me from acting on any drunken ideas I might have had to sneak over to Orion's.

NINETEEN

ORION

I ended up taking sleeping meds to prevent myself from hearing and/or spying on Dani's get-together. Thor slept like a champ for a solid twelve hours, so I got to sleep in the next day. The rhythm of the ocean outside my window a balm for my battered soul.

Before lunch, Thor and I walked to the small strip of beach where I did yoga for an hour, meditating and mentally running through my list of responsibilities. Reminded myself that the war in my head resulted from the war I had fought on orders from my country. I can't take the blame for the war or the attack. No longer an active Marine, my future stretched out impossibly far without the possibility of stepping into a war zone.

Trying to avoid obsessing over things that happened and keeping a healthy perspective seemed a constant struggle. Cognitive therapy helped me cleanse my mental palette, per se, when I had the sense to alter my perspective. For example, so long as I could stay as an observer, watching the incident play out, I could push through.

I remembered I needed to meet with my counselor today. A dreaded joy. What do I mean? She listens but asks hard questions. Not the kind I didn't have an answer to (although if I don't, she leads me until I do), but the soul-searching, reaffirming my existence-kind.

Lindsey Dent, my VA counselor, reminded me of a wise little owl with her stylishly cut silver hair and glasses that framed her dark brown eyes. During an earlier session in an unguarded moment, I commented on the comparison, upon which she responded: "Who, me?"

The corners of her lips turned up, and her eyes sparkled when she made a joke, no matter how corny. Her lightheartedness and humor reassured me during our first session, more than her tranquil gaze ever could.

"I ran into someone." I began, then shared my introduction to Dani.

"Sounds like her car struck yours, not the other way around." Lindsey smiled. "How did meeting her make you feel?"

"More alive than I've been in a long time."

"More than when you rescued Thor?"

Lindsey had been supportive of me keeping the dog. I had assumed she would have tried to talk me into searching for his previous owner, but she agreed with me taking him on as my responsibility. Must have thought it the best option.

"Yes, ma'am." I paused for a moment to consider my words. "Dani's like a new shade of color or an exotic wildflower that I've never seen before, and a fresh smell that overpowers everything else."

"Wow. Makes you pull out the fancy words. She's a veterinarian." Lindsey reminds me. "The ones I know have big hearts."

"Generous, yes... she's larger than life. Whenever she's around, I feel an unfamiliar joy and cheerfulness. She's letting me stay in her vacant cottage by the ocean while her brother repairs my Bronco."

Lindsey's forehead creased as I spoke. "You make that sound like a bad thing."

"I have never understood those kinds of people," I added.

Her gaze softened, and she leaned forward in her chair, closer to the camera. "Did you know that the veterinary profession has a high suicide rate? Maybe she finds it easier to wear a mask." Her gentle voice held an edge to it, as if warning me not to judge Dani.

I shook my head, unable to form words as Lindsey spoke again. "And lack of understanding shouldn't lead you to judge."

She knew me too well. But that's what made her the best therapist for me.

Before I could grumble that I hadn't judged Dani, Lindsey went on. She adjusted her glasses and cleared her throat. "During this first meeting in the veterinary clinic, did you deal with any anxiety?"

I nodded. "The smell and the florescent lights."

"Good. You identified several triggers. Disinfectant perhaps?"

"Yeah. Just like a human hospital."

"But you were in a clinic before with Thor with no issue."

She had a point. "Yes. But this time I believe my anxiety started after the car accident and escalated. Half a Xanax helped."

"Orion, I'm going to mention this so you keep it in mind in the future. Sometimes people who have had difficulties in their lives easily bond together. It's termed trauma bonding. It's phenomenal, really, the intense emotional attachment individuals can develop to each other.

"I'm sharing this because we've discussed it previously. You have that connection with your squad. When it happens, the comfort and connection can be intense and fast." She made a note or drew a doodle or whatever else shrinks do on their notepads.

We talked about surfing, my return to meditative yoga, and diet. There was something still lurking underneath the surface, an underlying fear that kept me from fully enjoying things. I knew she recognized it.

I rubbed my head, the stubble on my sides matching the stubble on my jaw.

"Are you still doing a lot of reading?"

"Not as much as before Thor, but yeah."

She dropped her chin, her brow furrowed. "I want you to give Dani a chance as a friend, Orion. Don't write yourself off as a bumbling idiot—it's not true. This is a great opportunity to make an important connection. Don't let it pass you by."

Then, as if on cue, she asked the question I dreaded. "Have you spoken to your family since your discharge?"

I shook my head, not meeting her gaze.

"You need to reach out to them, Orion," she said. "Your family is worried about you. Will always be worried about you. Let them know you're out and safe."

I wanted nothing more than to avoid it, but I knew that was only making the situation worse. I had to man up and rip off the metaphorical bandaid. Taking a deep breath, I replied, "I'll get there."

After the call with Lindsey, I felt restless. Her words echoed in my head; the struggle of veterinarians with mental illness weighed heavily on my conscience. I kept replaying the image of the semicolon tattoo on her wrist.

That symbol seemed a signal, a reminder, that even a person so vibrant might hide a deeper struggle within. Or perhaps the tat represented a friend or family member, someone else's mental illness.

The afternoon turned sunny and Thor and I walked around the property. A wood fence divided the patch of cropped grass, making a private area for the cottage. Dani's side of the fence opened up to a larger yard with an avocado and lime tree, a weeping willow, and several raised flower beds.

A pool and hot tub butted the back of the house. I hadn't seen them on the drive to the cottage because of the hedgerow. A screened back deck flowed into an enclosure of some sort. Vines crawled the welded stainless-steel cage with rounded corners and a roof. Inside were various perches, hanging toys, feeders, and nesting boxes.

Thor sniffed the perimeter while I peered more closely through the side. Nothing moved. Suddenly, a deafening squawk broke the silence, and I stumbled back in shock.

"Excuse me. Would you like to meet the birds?" A voice whispered from the shadows, making me jump.

A young woman, no, a teenager, stood beside me. She had intense blue eyes and a friendly smile.

I nodded, still trying to catch my breath. "Sure." I glanced at Thor, whose tail wagged in anticipation, then back to her. "What about him?"

"You can bring him, but please carry him."

"Lead the way," I said with a grin.

The young woman gave a toothy grin and gestured for us to follow her inside.

"I'm Sasha, by the way."

"Dani's neighbor?" I vaguely remembered her mentioning a daily visitor.

"Yeah. And you're Orion?"

"Rion."

"Cool. This is the aviary. We have Fleur back there. She's a twenty-five-year-old female Harlequin Macaw."

Sasha pointed near the far corner where a brightly colored parrot perched outside a large, pale wooden box. Bright orange feathers covered most of her body. Her wings started with green and shifted to blue flight feathers. Blue and green covered her back and head. She screeched, a deafening rrraaah. So here was the source of last night's birdcall.

Sasha continued, "She's saying hello."

A white bird flapped down from the ceiling and landed on Sasha's outstretched hand. She climbed up the girl's arm and tucked herself until the crook of Sasha's neck. The teen giggled. "This is Snow. She's a five-year-old Moluccan Cockatoo. And behind you," Sasha pointed.

Turned and found myself face-to-face with the smallest bird, a gray with piercing eyes.

"That's Timsy, an African Gray. She's seventeen."

"Peek-a-boo, pretty," Timsy said in a perfect, human-like voice. She clicked her tongue several times, wolf-whistled, and fluffed her feathers so she looked like a stuffed toy.

Behind me, Snow whistled and honked, her peek-a-boo call less defined.

Timsy bobbed her head and twisted, posing at me from one eye. Then she lifted a foot. "Up, dammit. I don't have all day."

Sasha laughed. "Oh no. Timsy and Snow are going to go to war for your attention."

I took a step back from Timsy's beak. It looked as sharp as any knife, and the bird moved toward me with a renewed interest, as if to say, "Are you my new friend?"

I felt my heart race as I moved closer to the door of the aviary, unsure of what to do. Snow flew around me and landed on a branch above Timsy, then eyed me. Fleur's sharp cries pierced the air, cutting through the warm humidity of the enclosure.

I wanted to be anywhere but in that aviary.

Thankfully, Sasha offered me a way out. "We should step outside before they get too riled up."

I nodded in agreement. Thor crawled onto my shoulder so he could get a better view of what was going on behind us as I walked out. I gave a quick look before stepping out. Fleur grabbed hold of a toy hanging next to her and vigorously shook it. I don't think my finger would have stayed attached to my hand if she grabbed it like that.

"Thank you for introducing me."

"No problem. I'm sure Dani will have them crawling all over you soon enough."

An image of all three birds perched on my head and shoulders while Dani murmured encouraging words in my ear struck my imagination. It made me chuckle because I realized that even in the darkness there was beauty to be found.

TWENTY

DANI

From the glass doors leading out to the back of the property, I watched Sasha walk around the deck after spending time with the birds. Orion and Thor were following her, which caught me off guard.

The door opened to let the sea breeze in as I made lunch, let in their chatter and I shamelessly spied on them. Thor approached Sasha, begging to be picked up. I counted the seconds until the teen gave in.

"You did great," she said as she bent to pick Thor up. He landed a brilliant tongue at her temple and started cleaning her ear. Sasha, to her credit, acted like a puppy slobbering up her face, was the most normal thing in the universe.

"I looked that nervous?"

She shrugged. "Dani's inside making lunch."

Orion's gaze flashed to the house, and I stepped back into the shadows, not wanting to get caught spying like a stalker.

He tucked his hands in the front pockets of his jeans that hugged his thighs. Thor sat in front of Sasha and lifted a front paw. Aroo.

Orion smiled at Shasha and turned as if he were leaving.

I yelled, "Rion! Hungry?"

I stood at the back screen door. Did I feel ridiculous with my hair in a messy top bun, dark-framed glasses on my windburned face, and a frilly apron over my tee and pink sweatpants? Not after I watched Orion's relaxed form. A smile slid onto his face as he saw me, and mine followed as easily as sliding into a warm pool of water.

Before he could form a response, his stomach answered for him loudly enough I heard it in the house. Sasha giggled and walked to the house.

"Hey, Danica," the teen said as they walked through French doors into my spacious kitchen.

Orion followed and seemed to ignore the decor—my white cabinets, whiter walls, and appliances with matte gold fixtures. His eyes were on me and not the dusky greens and dark browns that accented the area.

I swooped Sasha into a hug and kissed her on the top of the head. "How's my favorite daughter slash neighbor?"

"Good. Timsy and Snow like Rion."

My eyebrows lifted as he met my gaze. He wore a light gray tee with an image of a jackalope on it and hadn't taken his eyes off me since he walked in. I swore I could feel the heat of it on my skin. "Oh? Charming all the ladies around here, huh?" I lightly flung the end of a towel at Sasha, who had dropped onto a chair at the kitchen table. "Wash your hands and help me set the table." Then I pointed at Orion. "You, too."

"Yes, ma'am."

Sasha placed the back of her hand over her forehead in a dramatic fake swoon. "Pretty please teach Fleur manners like yours, Orion. Maybe she'll quit screaming when the phone rings."

"Sasha, Fleur will forever shriek. It's part of her charm," I said.

They washed their hands at the kitchen sink, chumming like old friends. I set out a bowl of water for Thor before pointing to the cupboards with dishes. He ambled over in his gangly puppy gait and shoved his snout down into the water to drink. Adorable and weird.

"Salad bowls, plates, glasses, please." I gave a friendly wink, hoping I didn't sound too demanding.

It pleasantly surprised me how relaxed he appeared around us. Gone was the Mr. Grumpy persona. Like a bashful toddler left without his mother, he withdrew from his shell while Sasha and I fell into our undemanding, back-and-forth that didn't require Orion to respond.

I explained, "Sasha helps me every day. She spends quality time with the parrots. As flock animals, they don't appreciate how little time I get with them. Sasha helps ease my absence." The sting that hit the center of my chest wormed up into my eyes, burning with building tears. How nice it would be to have an eight-to-five, or work from home. But wishing didn't fill an empty vessel. Hard work and opportunity will get me there some day.

Thor set out on his own adventure to inspect the wondrous scents in my house.

Soon enough, he came trotting back, his head careened over his shoulder. Not paying attention to where he was going, only to what might be behind him. He bounced off a chair and the fridge before he made it safely to my leg, where he plopped on my foot. His body quivered in fear or excitement. I gave him a reassuring head rub before he realized I wasn't Orion.

I knew, of course, the source of his discomfort. A very large, very fluffy, black monster cat sauntered around the corner as if basking in the sudden attention.

Look at me, peasants.

Rarrrr.

Bunnie's black hair transitioned to a thick pewter mane body with long black hairs extending from the tips of its ears like a bobcat. Intense amber eyes gleamed with spooky intelligence as if the creature could see the shape of your soul.

I said, "Hey, Bunnie. Did you meet Thor?"

His eyebrows reached for his hairline as he tried, unsuccessfully, not to chuckle. "Bunnie? It looks like a black lion."

Bunnie jumped gracefully onto the back of a chair, sat, and gazed out over the kitchen. Lion indeed. With a wide, powerful jaw.

"Any more pets?" he asked.

I poked Sasha with my elbow. "Nope. Sasha here is more than I can handle at times."

Sasha rolled her eyes.

As we cleaned up the dishes, I said, "Sorry to bug out. I've got a few appointments yet this afternoon."

Sasha waved as she left, the kitchen suddenly quiet.

Bunnie had vaulted off the chair, landing with a hushed gracefulness belying his size. He meandered between chair legs. I could hear his deep, rumbling purr from across the room.

Thor ran out from beneath his spot beneath Orion's chair suddenly, skidding to a halt in front of the cat. Bunnie lifted a front paw and meowed.

The puppy dropped and twisted his head, throwing a shoulder toward the cat. Bunnie's reach caught Thor above the eye. I swear to God—my cat petted his dog.

In the next blink, both were winding around each other, affectionate as two koi in a pond.

"Close your mouth, Rion. Bunnie is the kindest soul I know. Although if Thor tries to hurt him, Bunnie will kindly show him his attempt is futile."

I was in the act of dropping my sweatpants when Orion trained his blue eyes on me. Not to be concerned, as I had a pair of mesh jogging shorts underneath. "Not fulfilling your earlier request, hot guy," I said, pulling on my green work bibs. "Have a couple of horses to see."

He ran his tongue along his lower lip. "Oh? And what services do these horses require of you?"

"Dental work." I gazed off into space. The third visit this week. "Seems to be my week to do dentals."

"Really?" He wore an adorable, confused expression.

"There's room in the truck if you want to ride along. Thor's welcome, too." Dental work would be tame enough for him. Probably. If he agreed to go, would that mean because he wanted to spend time with me or learn about horse's teeth?

He stretched his muscular arms overhead. "I'll have to reschedule my afternoon..."

My eyes snagged on the exposed sliver of abdomen and heat flared low in my belly. I smiled. "I'd hate to cause you too much trouble." I pulled my zipper up, the sound cutting through Thor and Bunnie's playful banter.

twenty-one

ORION

Over the next couple of hours, we drove up into the mountains. Dani chatted with her clients on the phone like they were the most important of her oldest friends. Dani frequently flashed a quick, wide smile that wasn't forced or fake.

Any lull in conversation filled the vehicle with an easy quiet.

"Tell me a weird vet story."

"Oh," she tapped her finger on her lower lip. "Which one to pick?"

"That many?" I raised my eyebrows.

"How about one from this morning? On my way out to a horse emergency, a colic, which is a fancy term for bellyache, a client called about his upcoming appointment. I had the office call and let him know I was going to be late. Because of the emergency. Anyway, he screamed at me. Screamed! Because I didn't prioritize his visit."

"Really?" I've had to wait in doctor's offices before because of emergencies. It wasn't ideal, but shit happens. "So, what did you do?"

"I politely recommended he contact the office and speak with my boss. And he did. I sent her a message to give her warning."

"Don't leave me handing, Doc. What did she say?"

Dani made a brushing motion with her hands as if to rid them of crumbs. "She fired the guy."

"You can fire a client? Huh," I said, looking out the window at the dry, brown terrain. I noticed whenever her phone rang, her entire body tensed. "I have my ringer turned off. All my notifications, actually. I can't stand the noise. I suppose that's not feasible for you?"

"No. I kinda need my phone for work." She sighed. "What a novel idea, though. I turn it off when I am on vacation."

"What do you do for vacation?"

She chewed on the inside of her lip. "When was the last vacation? Hmm, I sleep?"

"Are you asking me?" I huffed out a disbelieving laugh.

"I don't get much free time. If I have a day or two off, I stick around home. I mean, I would love to take a week and go somewhere tropical. Or Iceland."

"Tropical or Iceland? Those are two very different locations."

Too soon the ride ended, and we arrived at her destination, a lovely horse barn built within a gated neighborhood. I have visited many fancy places in my travels, but the barn in which the horses waited seemed much too fancy for me to even set foot inside. The cobblestone alleyway, clean enough to eat off of, sprawled out before us, wide enough to drive a truck through. Heavy-looking, polished wood stall doors with roses carved into the surfaces lined the rows, and black horses, their manes braided and coats shining with fragrant oils, stuck their heads out as we walked through.

Dani explained on our walk through the barn that we were there to see two Warmblood geldings, top-dollar jumping horses, who were slated to ship to France next month.

Vaccinations, deworming, teeth, and sheath cleanings.

"Teeth, sheath, and shots." She wagged her eyebrows as she spoke.

A blush spread across her cheeks and as she turned her gaze away, and I admired her smooth hair, tawny colored, the ends lighter than the roots. She smiled, as if feeling my gaze. I suspected what the sheath part meant. Didn't quite understand why it needed cleaning.

At the high-end barn, a stable hand held the horses for her while I watched. He regarded my dog warily, but relaxed as Dani chatted amiably with him. Thor was safely on the end of a leash and more threatened by all the large horses.

With a modded-out DeWalt-like drill handle, the "float" Dani used for her dental work was a round flat bit at the end of a long shaft. It floated over the horse's teeth, shaving down the sharp points that had formed and prevented the horse from a full range of motion in the jaw.

After the dental while the gelding continued to snooze under the influence of chemical sedation, Dani set up for the sheath portion of the visit. She placed a bucket of warm water and a jar of powder on the ground where she stood next to the horse's side.

The stable hand, Jerry, talked on his phone the entire time.

"What are you doing now?" I asked, getting closer. I held Thor in my arms, worried he might piss on the floor and get us kicked out.

"This is the sheath part." Then, gloved, she reached beneath the gelding toward its back legs, and stuck her hand up into the pocket where the horse held its penis. Sorry. Not a pocket. The sheath.

I asked the question that had been lingering in my mind since I first heard about it. "Why?"

While focused on her work, Dani explained horses accumulated fluids, sweat and urine, that mixed with dirt, dead skin cells, et cetera, and formed smegma, which can layer in the preputial cavities and create beans in the urethral sinus.

"I've removed beans so large they were preventing the gelding from urinating." She held one out, a grayish-colored bean.

The stiffness I had from imagining she was handling my dick died at the thought of a stinky bean blocking me from taking a piss. Shit.

"You went to vet school to learn how to do this?" I laughed, feeling all shades of awkwardness besides the mandatory second-hand embarrassment for the horse who slept standing up.

"No. I went to vet school because I wanted to learn how to provide quality health care for animals. The sheath cleaning is a bonus talent."

Jerry took the time from his uber important conversation to say, "Make sure we can see ourselves in it when you're done, Dani."

I damn near choked on my laughter. Crude humor has a place everywhere, it seemed.

"Aye-aye, Captain," Dani said with a crooked smile. Then to me, she whispered, "He's a squid."

As I wondered why she would call Jerry a squid, she furrowed her brow, uncertainty creeping over her face.

"Don't you call Navy people squids?"

Her concerned look brought a smile of my own. "Yes, ma'am."

"Ooh, so gentlemanly." She rinsed the horse's fifth appendage, the tip disturbingly reminding me of a chocolate-dipped cone. "My brother told me you were a Marine." To Jerry, she said, "Okay, Jer. Next one."

Another hour later, as she cleaned her equipment, a beeping sounded. Dani checked her phone, then made a call.

"Looks like I have an emergency. You good to go with me to a laceration? A horse cut its leg. Possibly lots of blood." Her voice took on a higher pitch.

"Look. It's a bird. No, it's a plane," I teased, trying not to wonder what I'd be facing. "Nope. It's the incredible Dani, ready to swoop in and save the day," I declared with an exaggerated flourish.

"Sorry to burst your bubble. No superhero here," she quipped and rolled her eyes. Turning back to the handler, she said, "Send me a message tonight, Jer. Let me know how they are doing." She shut her vet box on the pickup box and slapped her palm on the back lid. "Off we go."

I walked to the passenger side. Jerry shook my hand, his smile as warm as the handshake. "I hope you are worthy of that happiness she's projecting. Dani deserves someone who treats her well."

I gazed at him steadily, needing to understand what he hadn't said. "I don't know if I'm good enough," I started, but he cut me off with a look.

"I don't know either, buddy. But just don't be like the last guy. There are a lot of folks who adore her and won't stand for her to be—" His hand tightened. A warning. Then he dropped my hand and sighed, his eyes growing pained. "How anyone could treat another so terribly?" Jerry shook his head, clearing the sudden rush of emotion. "You seem decent enough. Quiet. Considerate. Take care of her."

Jerry turned and walked away, leaving me unsettled. I should have told him I was just along for the ride. The double meaning wasn't lost on me. The moths lining my stomach began fluttering, awakening with a disturbing suspicion.

I climbed in the cab and found Dani on her phone. Thor crawled to the center and sprawled between us.

"I doubt I'll make it tonight. Tomorrow, though, I have off. I'll plan to head in for practice then." She paused as the other person spoke. "Awesome. Send me a bill." She hung up and threw me a dazzling smile. "My Mini is fixed."

I returned her grin. "That's great."

"Sorry. Yours isn't done." Her smile faltered, and she chewed on her bottom lip.

Shrugging, I dropped my gaze to Thor to avoid watching her mouth. He had rolled to his back, so I scratched his smooth belly. "Not a big deal. I don't have a deadline to be anywhere."

"Man, that sounds nice." She sighed.

Carry On My Wayward Son by Kansas came on the radio. Talk about radio luck—cue appropriate music.

"My last vacation was disguised as a CE meeting. Continuing education. In Vegas." She barked out a laugh, startling Thor. "Oh, sorry, baby." She rubbed his head, and he repositioned, stretching on his belly, resting his chin on her thigh.

If I had a magic lamp at that moment, I would have wished to trade places with Thor.

"But you have tomorrow off?"

She checked the road before turning off the highway into a gravel drive.

"Yeah. Get them every now and again."

The quiet that descended between us had a weary heaviness. I began humming along to the song, and I felt her smile from across the seat.

The next song, The Last Worthless Evening by Don Henley, came on. Dani sang, her voice soft, and I closed my eyes and joined her.

"The best kind of music is shared," she said during an instrumental break. "Sorry. Hope you don't mind my terrible singing. I'm used to driving alone. It's a good way to stay awake."

Her self-deprecating chuckle gnawed at me.

"Dani?"

"Hmmm?"

"You don't need to apologize. You have a lovely voice. And besides, this is your truck—"

"Work truck," she interrupted with a teasing lift to her mouth.

Momentarily distracted by her captivating profile, I imagine how they would feel against mine. I forgot about my damaged vehicle, my discharge, and my family. All my thoughts focused on the woman beside me.

Stray hairs curled at her temple and neck. Three moles formed a triangular constellation below her right ear adorned with three silver piercings, one stud and two tiny hoops. She smiled, as if feeling my steady gaze.

I cleared my throat. "Please stop apologizing. Honestly, I love that you sing along to the radio. Makes me comfortable to do the same." Badly, but still. As she drove, I asked, "So, why'd you become a vet?"

She pulled onto another gravel road that led up a hill. "I wanted to become a doctor like my dad, but, don't laugh, people ick me out."

"Not laughing. I get it." I thought I got it.

"I mean, I have to deal with the owners, but I don't have to examine them, ya know? Although I have had an owner ask for my opinion on their issues." She pulled in front of a ranch style home, plain compared to the barn we had recently visited, and drove around to the back where a small barn stood. "Okay, get your game face on, Orion. I want to warn you, there will be blood, so if you are a fainter, maybe hang back."

"You have a lot of people fainting on you?"

"I had a cop pass out cold while I castrated his horse. He knocked his head bad enough that he got a concussion. I would rather be safe than call an ambulance."

"Yes, ma'am."

I'm not one of those people who faint at the sight of blood. I am one of those humans who experiences panic attacks because of one of plenty on a laundry list of triggers. Should I have told her? Remembering my counselor Lindsey suggested spending time with Dani might help me transition from associating triggering hospital scents with my past to veterinary medicine of my present, I decided I would try it. I had meds along in case I needed a rescue from the heart-pounding cliff of anxiety.

A young man met us at the small wood barn and led us inside to where a horse, a young Friesian colt, stood quietly, eating hay. An older woman, one step shy of a corpse with her wispy silver hair and shriveled appearance, stood next to the horse. A good strong wind could pick her up and carry her away, never to be seen or heard from again.

Then she spoke, her lively recounting of the events leading to the horse's wound a vibrant contrast to her appearance. The young horse had attempted to jump over a fence and got hung up on a post.

Because of the dim interior and the horse's black coloring, I missed the blood covering his hind leg and congealed at his hooves. Dani looked over the wound, squatting near the front and craning her head beneath him with a flashlight. "Well, Lilian, I'm going to sedate Percy and get him cleaned up. From here, it looks like a good chunk of skin is pulled away from the inside of his thigh. The testicle looks intact. I'll get a better idea of the extent of the injury once I'm down there. Rion, do you mind helping me?"

So far, so good. The blood wasn't bothering me. Back at her truck, I followed her guidance. I filled a stainless-steel bucket with warm water and added a blue disinfectant while Dani pulled out ampules of drugs, needles, and syringes. She had a pack wrapped in blue paper that she placed in a supply caddy along with sterile gloves, regular gloves, cotton, and an assortment of leg bandage materials. She talked me through everything, keeping my mind occupied with the task at hand.

"So," she said when she had her supplies ready, "you feeling like you can assist?" Her eyes were hopeful and excited. "Thor can hang out in one of the empty stalls while we work, safely out of harm's way. It will take me a while. I'll have to clean it, debride it a bit. That's just a fancy word for thorough cleaning to freshen the edges. Then I'll suture it from inside to out, place a drain, wrap his leg below the injury to prevent swelling and wrap the opposite leg as well. Horses." She gave a one shoulder shrug as she surveyed the back of her truck as if searching for something she may have missed. Then she shook her head once. "Right. I've got antibiotics and pain meds. We are good to go. Ready?"

Standing beside her, her arm brushed against me, and her warm scent filled my lungs. At the moment, I felt like I could tackle anything that came my way.

Dani chatted with Lilian, the owner, while she sedated the colt, Percy. Within minutes, he became sleepy, his head dropping in slow increments. The man, Cam, held the horse.

While cleaning the wound, Dani narrated what she found, letting us know how the wound looked and what supplies she needed from me. Like she had with Thor, I realized she did this to compartmentalize the process mentally. When I suggested she used more sciency words, she looked up at me, the glare of her headlamp blinding. I squinted and held a hand up to block the migraine-inducing light.

"Oh, sorry," she said, and toggled the light off. "More sciency?" Her slight grin, unsure and questioning.

Did I mention they would be a distraction? "Yeah. You're a doctor. Use your big doctor words."

"Most people prefer simplified terms." She chewed on her bottom lip, probably wondering why I asked. Her green eyes appeared black in the shadow of the sedated horse.

"Not me. You make them sound sexy." Trying not to groan at my idiot self, I instead offered her a bold smile. Those smile things were beginning to feel good around her.

She tilted her head, her mouth gaping prettily. Then she said, "oh," and turned back to her work, not before I saw the flush on her cheeks.

And she used big words that flustered me like a little school kid. Damn. Who knew intelligence could be so sexy?

The work allowed me to focus on something other than the coppery tang of blood and dry heat of an unseasonably warm late fall Cali afternoon. She worked in a difficult position and dangerous one, crouched at his hind leg opposite the injured one, halfway beneath the horse's belly. Foaled in February, the Friesian was already quite big, although bony and gangly and looking like a teen growing faster than he could eat. Dani put her complete trust in Cam to monitor the horse, and the horse to tell her how he fared with her ministrations. She had rolled her sleeves and my sight caught on her graceful hands, and their meticulous, methodical motions. The flex of her muscles. The blue of her veins.

A steady, albeit slow, stream of blood flowed down his leg and pooled at his hoof. It blended with the horse's ebony coat in the shadows that Dani's headlamp failed to reach. The sharp aroma of the disinfectant mixed with alfalfa hay, fresh manure the colt had dropped before we arrived (thankfully Cam shoveled it away before Dani got to work), and the sweet smell of the horse himself. I picked out those small details to focus on. Like how his coat glistened with sweat and white foam developed on his flank and over his shoulder.

Every once in a while, the colt would startle, his head jerking. Dani explained part of his sedation caused ticks and reminded Cam to not stand directly in front of the horse.

She sutured a tube through the center of the wound to allow drainage, then hosed the leg off. When at last she was ready to wrap the horse's legs, I took a deep breath. My mind flipped through the sequence of events, of Dani's work that patched up the injured horse. Throughout the procedure, she threw her used materials in a bucket lined with a garbage bag.

I helped her clean up. The air had cooled considerably, thanks to the mountains, and a chill touched my damp skin. She disposed of her sharps and washed her hands. As I pulled out the bag of garbage, a whiff of blood struck me like a punch to the chest. Darkness gathered around me and I heard voices as if my ears were stuffed with cotton.

Back in my nightmare, I saw bits of camouflage fabric doing a macabre dance across the dry earth, swaths of blood painted along in their wake. The spots grew and coalesced, flowing toward my shoes, and toward the pickup's tires. I stepped back, knowing I couldn't let my boots contact the vile liquid.

Something touched my arm, and I jerked back. Bile burned a path up my throat.

"Orion."

I was underwater, drowning now. Unable to breathe. The light too bright. My chest too tight.

"Orion."

I blinked, gasping for air. Dani gripped my arms, clinging fiercely, her worried face staring up into mine.

"Breathe with me."

I focused on her mouth. The rise and fall of her chest. The curve of her collarbone.

In. Out. In. Out.

She cupped a hand on my cheek, her green eyes dark, staring at me with a beautiful intensity. The pinch in my chest relaxed, but the moths in my stomach alighted, fluttering a chaotic rhythm. Silence seemed to connect us in the way words never could. My vulnerability was on sharp display, my soul ragged and craving her comfort while my mind demanded I flee.

Run.

Get lost.

"Orion."

My name on her tongue sounded like a prayer. Her palms moved up and down my arms. Something to focus on.

A dry mouth makes for terrible conversation, and I couldn't work up enough saliva to speak, so I gave her a quick nod. I'm okay.

Dani gave my arms a squeeze and searched my face, as if to make sure I was being truthful. Whatever she saw made her step back, releasing me.

"Why don't you go get Thor? I'll finish up here."

Cam had already led Percy into the stall next to Thor. The horse stood, head down, both hind legs wrapped in white and orange bandages. He held Thor, rubbing the pup's head as I approached.

"Cute dog. Weimaraner?" he asked.

I nodded, still not able to speak.

Seventies music played on the way back into town. The rock and roll acted like a balm, soothing my nerves. Dani made a few phone calls but said little between the exchanges. I was good with it, preferring not to talk about what had happened.

TWENTY-TWO

DANI

As we neared town, my inner voices became overwhelming. *Talk to him! Ask him what was bothering him! Do something to get his mind off whatever dragged him down!*

I chided myself for putting Orion through the laceration experience. I should have known better. He should have told me. Those two thoughts neither made the situation better, nor could change the past.

So, I said, "Wanna hear a story?"

Orion had been looking out the side window, absently stroking Thor's head, but he turned and caught my eye.

I gave him a wide grin. "It's a story about bad choices and survival."

He sniffed. The barest of curves at the corners of his full mouth. Stubble shadowed his jaw and I had the urge to brush my thumb across his lips and chin, skim across the contrasting surfaces.

"Not long ago," I began, "one of my equine clients brought in her Great Dane for me to see on emergency."

"Because Great Danes are the same size as ponies?" he quipped.

I recalled the appointment with a clarity one has for fond memories: crisp images of the person and animal involved, the coldness of the exam table as it dug into my hip, the actions I took, but everything else, the noise and bustle around me, were fuzzy.

"So this woman brought in a Great Dane for vomiting. Arlo. And yeah, he was as large as a miniature horse. Classic Scooby coloring, fawn with a black mask instead of the black spots. The owner insisted on rads, sorry, radiographs or x-rays of the dog's abdomen."

"I'm good if you use the big words, Dani. You sound intelligently sexy, not condescending, and it makes you more desirable."

His quip made my stomach flutter. For a moment, I forgot what I had been saying. I slowed the vehicle to turn a corner. The motions–turning the blinker, checking my mirrors–allowed me enough time to screw my head back on. "During my exam, Arlo slobbered a bit. Dry heaved a few times, but his belly wasn't sensitive to palpation. All in all, his exam didn't show any reason for the acute vomiting. She shared that Arlo had even vomited on the drive in. Didn't really give a straight answer as to when it started." I scratched the itchy skin behind my left ear as I turned a street corner. "Now, usually I wouldn't get too excited over the timeframe of the dog's status. I mean, not every vomiting dog is an emergency, right? Sometimes it passes. Mr. Scooby Dane was bright and alert, acting all normal. But I trusted this client to know her pet. She was very careful and knowledgeable about her horses, so I did as she asked. I took the rads. Guess what I found?"

Orion shrugged, seemingly hanging onto my words, or mesmerized by the acorn-shaped air freshener hanging from the rear-view mirror. At my lengthy pause, he turned and met my gaze. A tingling warmth spread through me that had nothing to do with the California sun.

Eyes back on the road, I pulled into a parking spot and cleared my throat. "Nothing! I headed back into the exam room with the dog. Showed the owner the radiographs. When I pointed out all the major landmarks and nothing stoodout as the cause of the dog's condition, the woman broke down. Full-on ugly crying. All the while clutching her large purse to her chest." I ran a hand over my face to stop the smile that was breaking out.

"I didn't know what to do. Had a minute where I questioned her life choices and how I could help. I ended up patting her back while rubbing the dog's monstrous head. Finally, the owner rummages in her purse on the exam table and pulls out a shoe box. The Dane perks up, his tail wagging so hard his back half swayed. Arlo started to lean into me. Hard.

"Nestled inside among a pile of paper towels were three baby squirrels. Very new. Their eyes weren't open, and their ears were flat against their soft little heads. 'These were the only ones I could save,' the woman says. *The only ones she could save.* She also mentioned that there was another dead one in the vehicle. The one he had puked up on the ride in."

I saw in my periphery that Orion was hanging on my words.

"I mean, how do you tie a vomiting dog to newborn squirrels? Right?" I threw him a wide grin.

Incredulity slowly morphed into delight, and he flashed me an honest grin, one that crinkled the corners of his baby-blue eyes. "He ate them?"

"Uh-hmm. Turns out Arlo sniffed out a squirrel's nest and gulped down six babies." I was laughing now, my eyes watering, "and then puked them all back up. Three lived. Survived! From being in the belly of a Great Dane."

"You're serious? Three lived?"

I nodded and turned to face him. Now that we were parked, my hands jumped into the story. "I saw her a few months later. At her horse barn. She kept the baby squirrels. Hand-raised them. They were beloved by everyone at the stable and even rode around on Arlo's back. She gave me this," I tapped the air freshener, a familiar thing inside the truck that had hidden in plain sight.

He barked out a laugh, a full body shake. Thor hustled up and jumped on him, his tongue flagging as he tried to lick Orion's face.

I felt lighter after seeing him laugh. Dwelling on the bad stuff for too long led to worse shit. I had enough of that without adding a tablespoon more. There was good to be found in every situation, even in the embrace of shadows. Other times, I've found I need to become the light and break free from the dark, if only for a short while.

I parked my vet truck behind the strip mall outside the garage door. A hot dry blast welcomed me as I stepped out of the air-conditioned truck and onto the black pavement. Why the world hadn't started using color to break apart the heat-intensifying substances that covered parking lots and roads, I'll never quite understand. With all the carbon footprint talk, surely the dark surfaces only added to global warming.

Orion and Thor followed me through the backdoor into the storage area of our building space. Orion watered Thor while I restocked. We were the only people in the clinic, although the muffled barks of kenneled patients in the next room announced our arrival.

Beneath the gruff exterior, I recognized a kindred spirit. For a few moments when he allowed it, anyway. Of course, the panic attack had coiled tightly, a stranglehold of memories unwilling to let him go. Like ex-lovers hellbent on tormenting him for eternity, whatever demons that darkened his starry nights and chilled his bones hung over him like a dark cloud. Did he fear his next attack? I hadn't asked if he had medication to help him.

That was how he relaxed before when I first met him. The realization resounded in my hollow chest. It was one thing to wear internal scars of your own, but to learn of another's was a reminder I wasn't the only one with struggles. Wasn't alone.

What had he experienced? War. Life. Nothing compared to hers, surely, but comparing horrors wasn't a healthy idea. Would airing his internal troubles make them less potent? When she finally shared hers with a counselor, Katey, and her family, much of the hefty weight lifted, the weight shared between them. Keeping them stored internally only allowed their power to grow, consume her mind, and taint every good thing that came along.

Should I ask him if he took any medication, or if he needed some? God, no. Thinking about how I would react to that made me realize the best I could do was to be present. Compassionate.

Whenever I caught his eye, I gave him what I hoped was an honest smile without pity. He responded with one of his half-cocked smirks that edged on inappropriate. The man was a lesson in contrasts. One minute he was a grumpy ass, the next he was sweet, and the next he was barely keeping himself together.

I had no room to complain, much less comment. My experiences taught me to wear a smile when inside my shriveled heart and soul banged relentlessly against a chest cavity void of hope. Time had pumped hope and dreaming back into my chest. After all, the only guarantee in life was the moment at hand.

Maybe the girls were right. I needed to let loose. Give in to my temptations. Ask for what I want. How else could I learn what I like? Except that nagging voice in the back of my head pointed out, "How will it feel when you discover all men are like Darius? That you failed?"

I hated that voice in my head. But... it had a point. What if I'd never be enough for someone? Wasn't it satisfactory that I finally found myself worthy of my own love, at least on most days?

I prayed that Orion's intentions were pure. Who am I kidding? I didn't. I realized I would very much like to be ravaged by him. Revered. Worshiped.

Two shelving units out of sight of my visitors, a box of cotton pads gave up quite a fight, sneaking away with each minor touch of my fingertips, evading my reach on an upper shelf. It didn't elude me that much of my life was like that frigging box... out of reach. Peace and quiet... out of reach.

Calm within my soul... out of reach. Someone to love me unconditional-
ly... Bunnie.

I hopped several times. Looked for the step stool while I palmed my forehead. Seriously, why was life suddenly being a bitch? I recently purchased
three step stools just to ensure one was always available. Where the hell
were they?

My heart beat faster and I felt the corner of my eyebrow twitch. Great.
Add low potassium to my list. I inhaled, counting to four. Whispered,
"Calm down." Got pissed for hearing myself say *calm down*.

Orion stepped up, warmth coiling off his brawny body. "Can I help
you?"

My maniacal laugh escaped. "I don't know. Can you?" Flexing my fists
at my side, I counted a few more breaths.

Orion stood next to me, not touching me, but not moving away from
my crazy. *Warning: Danger Orion Windwalker. You are in the danger
zone.*

I was losing it. Like my brain decided it was my turn after witnessing
Orion struggle twice now. *You're up, doc.*

Breathe.

When I regained a semblance of balance, I said, "I just need that box of...
things." His closeness flustered me. As much as my inability to reach the
box. I couldn't recall what I needed, or what they were called. The fluster
intensified as he leaned in and up, lifting his arm to grab the meddlesome
box. A faint odor of spicy men's deodorant wafted over me, and I felt my
undies turn into a slip-n-slide.

Ask for what you want. Right. "I want you to have dinner with me." I
breathlessly stumbled over my words, baby-stepping with a mild case of
rush. I want you to have dinner with me? Way to bumble fuck 'I want you'
and 'will you have dinner with me.'

He dragged his tongue over his lower lip, watching me intently.

"I mean, would you join me for a late dinner?" I smirked hoping I came
across as playful, and not as a jaunty yearling colt.

His mouth curved up, dazzling me. He opened his mouth to say something, but the sound of water running nearby drew our attention away
from each other. Thor had taken that moment to pee on the doorstep.

TWENTY-THREE

ORION

I examined my haggard face in the mirror. The afternoon had been a boon and a bust. I managed not to have a full-scale panic attack, but Dani witnessed my near fall. What would she think of me, of my weakness? She invited me for supper. That was a good thing, right?

Beneath her perky exterior, I had glimpsed a certain darkness, although the extent and kind remained to be seen. Her calm in the face of my storm suggested she was accustomed to demons of the mind.

Or perhaps she was that empathetic.

Exhaustion pulled harder at me than gravity, but I was desperate not to be alone. Although Thor was a splendid companion, the more time I spent around Dani, the more I craved her company. Normally, that doesn't happen. I barely stood myself for too long, much less another person I just met.

After a quick shower, I shaved and pulled on a pair of fairly clean jeans and a black tee. Thor and I walked back to her house to find her grilling on the back terrace, a cold beer bottle in her hand, and a relaxed smile on her pretty face. One bird squawked from the enclosure nearby upon my approach and Dani looked up.

String lights hung between the pool and the deck, casting her in a warm glow. She looked iridescent, a diaphanous creature that might have easily escaped from another realm. Would I scare her away?

I sniffed and looked away. Apparently, I had been reading too many fantasy books of late.

She closed the grill lid and walked to meet me.

"Here ya go, Rion." She extended a beer. "Unless you would like wine or—"

"Beer is good." I clinked my bottle with hers. "Cheers."

"Cheers."

She had showered as well, her damp hair hung heavily down her back. Mascara darkened her eyelashes and there was a pink tint on her lips, deeper than normal. She wore a strappy white cotton dress. Her long, shapely legs were bare, with Birkenstocks on her feet.

"You are beautiful, Dani."

Her skin turned a precious shade roses would be jealous of. "You're funny. I hope you don't mind." She chewed on her lower lip. "I've been wearing coveralls for so long. I wanted to, I don't know... not." She chuckled.

I followed her into the house and into the cavernous living room. Bunnie watched me with golden eyes, the tip of his tail twitching as he rested like a king in front of the fireplace. The flames danced behind him from the gas-lit fire.

Bunnie had the most insanely majestic, dare I say, God-like look. Not the smooth-coated angular Egyptian deities but the haughty, "You should count yourself fortunate if I allow you to touch me," or "If I deem you worthy of consumption, peasant, you shall rejoice in my feasting on your meager soul."

Maybe my next journal entry should be *The Life of Bunnie*. I could visualize the stress reduction as a sheen of oil oozing from my pores. Again, too many fantasy books.

"The potatoes have a bit to cook. What are you up for? Watch a movie. Find a book to read and veg with my cat? Sit and stare at each other until we come up with something to talk about? Help me prep the rest of the food?"

Thor had wandered over to the fireplace and was trying to climb up next to Bunnie. The cat watched, tail twitching.

"I think Thor is claiming Bunnie." Claiming. The word made funny tingles break out in my gut. I turned to Dani, thinking. Calculating. Hanging around her was easier when a horse wasn't bleeding out next to us. I said as much.

"First of all, I want to apologize. Wait. Should I apologize?" She tilted her head to the side as she considered me.

Held in place by her gaze, I said, "No need to apologize. I'd rather you didn't treat me like a weak damsel."

"That's too bad. I have the cape and everything."

"Would you be willing to wear the cape and nothing else?"

It was her turn to give me an assessing look. "I don't think you are ready for that yet, Rion."

It would be a shame to not prove to her I was very much, in fact, ready for all of her.

TWENTY-FOUR

DANI

As I chopped onions next to the sink, Orion came up behind me. My mind insisted someone else towered behind me and I responded by stiffening. My pulse pounded inside a tightened chest while my gut churned. I struggled for air.

Whether he picked up on these changes, I don't know. I wanted to run far from him as much as I wanted to turn into him. Two warm hands descended on my upper arms and squeezed.

"Need any help?" His low, sexy voice and hot breath curled around my ear, and I felt the rumble in his chest travel the length of my spine.

I needed so, so much help. Bright flashes of light obscured my vision, and I flinched when his arms came around me. Still, I didn't say anything. A whimper escaped me, my throat constricting.

"Dani. Would you like me to step away from you?"

My mind fumbled for a response. *Do I want him to move away?* I closed my eyes as his thumbs brushed across the inside of my wrists. A strange thing happened then. The fear melted away, replaced by relief. Peace.

I leaned my shoulders into his chest. "No."

His chest rumbled with a sound of approval. "I'm going to take the knife and help you cut. Okay?"

Body still mostly frozen, I nodded.

"Rest your hands on mine, baby."

Following his request, I placed my hands atop his. As he sliced the onion, I focused on his hands... the way they moved and held the knife, the onion. The neat curves of his short fingernails. The three freckles on his right thumb knuckle.

In a conversational tone, as if I wasn't falling apart in his arms, he said, "Tell me something, Dani. If you could do anything instead of being a vet, what would you do?"

The unexpectedness of his inquiry allowed me to draw in a deep, slow breath, and my heart rate slowed. I felt unsteady on my feet as I forced a slower exhale, the warmth of relief radiating from within.

This was real. He was real, not the nightmare Orion/Darius. A sob threatened to escape, and I desperately tried to think of his question. The simple answer sat at the forefront of my brain. I could picture the storefront, the colors, the scents.

My eyes burned, and I blinked, but couldn't hold back the tears. My nose began running. Orion sniffed. It seemed the onion had taken effect on both of us, its organosulfur compounds wreaking havoc on our tear ducts. We were Onion Crying.

Not wanting to lift my hands to backhand my tears, they coated my cheeks.

"Um. Cupcakes." I cleared the frog from my throat.

"Hmm. Cupcakes. Expand."

His brief command, gentle and curious, allowed more of the tension to bleed from my shoulders.

"A cupcake store. Not one that sells pretty cupcakes, though."

Slice. Slice.

"A mashed cupcake."

"Like a cake pop?"

"Exactly. But on a requested basis. There would be six revolving flavors of cake and icing. The customer would make their selections, with or without a vanilla bean gelato add-on. Then it would be dipped in a candy coating before serving."

Slice. Slice.

"Orion." I turned my head, and my skin brushed his whiskers. "The onion is sliced enough."

With me glued to his front, we sidestepped to the sink where he washed our hands. His skin slid across mine in the warm, sudsy water causing electricity to tingle up my arms and deep into my chest. When my hands were dried with the dish towel, he stepped away before I could turn into him.

Not that I wanted to do it more than anything in my life.

"Mash Cakes? Sounds like a place I would hang out."

"Hang out?" I reached for a paper towel, wiping my tears.

"Yeah. Read from the selection of books on hand. Make love-struck eyes at the server."

A surprised laugh choked out of me. "Rude."

He faced me, leaned a hip into the counter, crossed his arms, and wrinkled his nose. "I just assumed you would be the server. Wearing a cute, ruffled apron." He reached over and rubbed a strip of the ruffle on the apron I wore between his fingers.

"Oh?" The timer beeped, indicating I needed to get the steaks on the grill.

He leaned forward and in a conspiratorial whisper said, "Dr. Lavigne, I happen to know a super-secret, killer chocolate cake recipe."

I resisted the urge to trace the silhouette of his face. "Do you? And how do I go about getting access to such an incredible recipe? To steal and use in my cupcake store, that is?"

He leaned in closer still, his freshly shaven cheek brushing mine. I inhaled, my eyelids closing as his heavenly musk filled my lungs.

His lips were soft on my ear as he said, "Sleeping with me would be a good start."

"Sleeping?" I arched an eyebrow I'm certain would have a certain Duke envious.

Orion brushed his nose against mine before softly rubbing our lips together. "Among other things," he said before kissing me.

It was a soft, tentative kiss. Testing. And ended all too soon.

His dark eyes raged like a storm over the Pacific that would wash away my past and clear a path for the future. A shudder ran through me as I stared back as the what-ifs flooded my thoughts. What if Darius showed up? What if he hurt Orion? What if Darius made good on his promises and finished me? What if I stopped this now before it went further? What if I didn't?

"Dani?"

I blinked and refocused on Orion at the sound of his whispered word.

"Get out of your head for a while. Come back to me," he murmured.

I cleared my throat.

"Did you just growl at me?" His wry smile made my insides turn to goo.

I squeezed my eyes tight. "No. Yes. I, ah, sometimes make a weird grunting hum. Yeah. Maybe. I'm back." I stepped away, clapped my hands, and said, "Time to get the steaks on the grill."

"Dani. I won't hurt you. Ever." His expression had morphed into one of sincerity.

My chest constricted, and I gave him a sad smile. "Rion, I think you sell yourself short."

ORION

It turned out conversation with Dani continued to be easy. Like her, the food was perfect, but I already knew she would taste even better.

I learned her father, Gavin Lavigne, had been a top obstetrician in his practice until his semi-retirement. Now he traveled for seminars as a guest speaker. Her mother, Ariadne Creswell, was *the* Creswell in the prominent law firm, Creswell & Hobbes, who had offices in San Diego, Los Angeles, and San Francisco.

"I'm adopted. My dad had a patient, a pregnant teen. She, my birth mother, Lorraine, was unable to raise me. My parents already had Elliot and Eamon, but they were struggling to get pregnant again. My dad suggested adopting me." She laughed, then took a sip of her beer. "It never bothered them having a kid with different colored skin. I, on the other hand, went through a phase where I used to spend as much time outside, burning more than tanning, trying to be dark like my brothers."

Dani showed me a family picture that sat on the fireplace mantle. I didn't see contrasting skin colors, and Dani wasn't the only lighter-skinned person in the photos. I saw a happy family. A wave of homesickness struck me. I knew I should message them. Email. Something. But I still wasn't ready to face them.

"Elliot's boys and Eamon's daughter all wrestle." She rambled on. "I was going to help with practice tonight, but with the emergency, it got too late. I rescheduled for tomorrow."

"Wrestling? You help a lot?" I eyed her muscular frame with a fresh eye. She had a fit physique. I knew she ran, but wrestling? My interest peaked higher.

Dani nodded. "I wrestled in high school, back when girls and guys wrestled together."

"I wrestled, too."

Her grin widened in delight. "Were you any good?"

"I did okay. I'd be happy to have a wrestle-off."

She threw her head back and laughed. The light sound and the curve of her neck mesmerized me.

"I like it when you tease. You are a very intense person, Orion." When her humor evaporated, she asked, "Are you feeling better?"

And so, the topic arrived. I nodded.

"Do you want to talk about it?"

She had witnessed an unstable moment and brought me back from the precipice without the benefit of medication. I realized I didn't want her to see me as a delicate person, struggling with demons eating away at my mind. I wanted to be strong. Resilient. Powerful.

Right then, I was neither of those things and it angered me. "Not really." I followed her back to the kitchen and sat at the table.

She lowered herself in the chair across from me. "What's your family like?" She pulled her knees up and curled around them, resting her chin on one knee. She rolled a spoon handle between her fingers.

"My parents, Carson and Kira Windwalker, were both career military. Marines. Instead of dragging their kids all over the country when we got older, they left us with my grandparents. Garrett and Marie Voight. I'm the youngest of three. All military. Jeremy is the oldest. Married to his childhood sweetheart, Mia. They live near DC with three kids. Jax, Ethan, and Kade. Then there's my sister, Kya, stuck on a carrier somewhere in the Pacific. She's divorced, no kids. Then there's me."

"The baby, like me."

I raised my bottle in a salute.

"And you're a Marine. How long have you served?"

"A little over twelve years."

"Wow. Thank you so much for your service."

Her scent had settled in the backdrop, and I suddenly craved another sniff of the combo of fresh-baked cookies and exotic musk. I wanted to eat her and fuck her.

As if feeling my stare, she smiled and looked at me.

When folks thanked me, a barrage of emotions swept through. Pride, appreciation, embarrassment, humility. I hadn't served for any other reason than I felt it was expected, so I said as much. "It wasn't like my family pressured me into following the three generations before me who served. Although perhaps they did, in a way. Their questions about what I was planning for my future were like, 'Are you going to go into the Marines like your parents or another branch?' I was, am, a fitness buff. And was always a bit of a dreamer. Becoming a writer or a dog trainer was something I would do after I did my twenty years." I shrugged. "The Marines gave me a larger family and specific purpose in life." And now, I've lost that and don't know what to do, I didn't add. Melancholy struck me like a freight train, hard and fast, grabbing my breath away.

"Let me tell you a story." Dani leaned back in her chair, dropped one leg to the floor, and began. She pulled her skirt over her knee and fingered the hem as she spoke. "Once upon a time, a young girl fell in love with a boy in college. The boy was everything she wanted. He was funny, smart, kind, and doted on her. They got married when the girl got accepted into vet school."

A suspicion about this guy settled into my gut, and as she spoke, it hardened and began to burn.

Dani gazed at a point beside and beyond me, eyes unfocused as she succumbed to memories. I felt a bit like a voyeur, taking in every subtle detail. A chip in the outside corner of her top right incisor. The slight wrinkles at the creases of her eyelids. Faint purple smudges beneath her eyes, a mossy green at that moment. The way her forearm flexed as she peeled the label off her beer bottle.

"I graduated, and the happy bubble popped. If I'm being honest, the perfect relationship had been ringing the drain all of vet school. Maybe even at the start. The distraction of class and lab and clinics and work made it harder to grasp.

"My first job was near his hometown." She mentioned a town in Wisconsin. "My dream was to work on horses and exotics." A rueful smile curved her lips, and she returned her focus to her beer bottle. "Not a lot of horses and exotics in the area, so I turned to mixed animal rural practice. It wasn't very lucrative, and the hours were pretty much twenty-four/seven. I hadn't realized how much he had alienated me from my family by then. He became jealous of my work. Called and messaged me all the time. Showed up at work nearly every day. I was burning out on the job and my marriage. I wanted kids. He didn't." She paused for a long pull of her beer, then gestured her empty bottle in my direction.

After she brought us another fresh bottle, she went on.

"The emotional abuse leaves pretty thick, invisible scars. No one knew. When he started being, um, physically abusive, I struggled. A lot. Mentally.

"There I was. A doctor. Smart. Independent. Capable of anything. Capable of anything except admitting to myself that my partner had slowly and insidiously trapped me in a fucking cliche. I was a battered woman.

"Pride held me back for a long time. That and anxiety, depression, suicidal thoughts."

Ah, shit. The semicolon tattoo on the inside of her wrist... was for herself and not one of those awareness tats. I had a great desire to beat the guy within an inch of his life. Repeatedly.

She placed her bottle on the table and leaned forward, her eyes misty. "You already know the ending. The girl got out. But not by herself. No, I didn't finally have an epiphany and acknowledge my strengths. A coworker found me at my lowest point. She took me home. Let me sleep on her couch until I got myself situated."

She finger-wiped the tears from her eyes. As much as I wanted to hurt the man who put her through hell, I wanted more to go to her, pull her into my arms, and offer her whatever comfort I could.

"So, the moral of that story, Orion, is that I know how it feels to be embarrassed about where life ends up. There's nothing wrong with accepting help. Nothing weak about asking for help. It means you're facing your problems head-on." She shifted in her chair. "If you decide to stay for a while until you and Thor are in a better situation, that isn't because of my pity. It's you taking the time and effort to build yourself back up. And what better place than near the ocean?"

Dinner had been wonderful. Excellent food. Conversation. The cold beers relaxed me. Even she seemed to be more at peace.

She still smiled a lot, but I noticed a difference. They were softer. Genuine. Implied limitless opportunities. And I wanted to kiss her more.

What could I say in response to her comments? It wasn't like she had faked her happiness before. Not entirely. Although from her tale, it was pretty clear she learned how to do it well enough. Her smile was like her clothing. Not a mask, but a type of armor.

I recognized it because it was something I did. In contrast, my armor was in being quiet. Out of the way. Unseen. Or growly so people avoided me.

"So... you see me?" I said, feeling an unwelcome ache in the back of my throat. The words spilled out before I realized what I was saying. Of course, she did. Her telling her story was meant for me to understand I'm not the only one with baggage.

Her elbows rested on the table, arms crossed. Her eyes darkened to a haunted emerald and met mine unwavering. A subtle shift in the mood punctuated her gaze. The teasing tone had fled and, in its place, settled a sensual tension.

"I see you." She took a drink from the dark bottle, finishing her beer. "What now?"

"I feel like being a bad girl. Do you like bad girls?"

A glorious red hue bloomed across her collarbone, kissing her shoulders, and moved up her neck to her cheeks. Nervous?

"I, ah... are you... do you—?" *Was she into me?* I held a 95% confidence she was. My throat felt tight and I cleared it. "You are not a bad girl. But we could pretend."

"Well, I'm no princess." She huffed and wrapped her arms around herself.

I needed to say something to keep her attention on me. "Isn't there a song? Every princess needs a good fuck. Every bad guy needs some love?"

Her full lips spread back into a smile. "Yeah. That's not how it goes."

"No, I'm pretty sure that's exactly how it goes."

"Doesn't matter. I'm no princess."

"Aren't you though?" I gave her upper half the once over. "You are incredible. Not even the same caliber as me."

"Oh?"

"But I would love nothing more right now than to slide my clip into your chamber."

Her bright laughter broke through the rising awkwardness and illuminated my soul.

I grinned my *come hither* grin and lifted my chin in a slight invitation or a dare. I wasn't sure yet if I hoped she would rise to accept either. The promise of forgetting, for a little while, seemed like something we could both use.

She stood and walked around the table, holding my gaze.

I knew fear intimately. It coated my heart, filled the cracks and fissures from the dreaded trauma and agony of loss, and fortified my walls to keep people out while I healed.

No one needed to know the extent of my broken mind, and yet I saw a reflection in her eyes. Saw a hesitant woman. A scared girl. Scarred but resilient. Wild. Lonely. Not empty but wanting to be full.

I said, "Come here."

When she reached me, I felt the warmth of her slide over me. She placed her hands on my shoulders, pressing my back to the chair as she straddled my lap. Her fingers laced through my hair.

I hadn't been ready for anything so much as I was ready for her. Her thighs were smooth and firm. I skimmed my hands up her legs, beneath her skirt. Her grip tightened. She held me back, her face inches from mine.

"I see you. And I want you, Orion."

"Thank fuck because I want you, too." My palms cupped her *bare* ass. "You aren't wearing any underwear." I nudged my pelvis forward, rubbing along her center. I could feel her heat through my jeans.

"Would you believe I'm all out of clean ones?" She said, her breath hot as it brushed against my skin.

"No." I pictured her delicate inner thighs chafed by my whiskers, which only made the blood pump harder into my groin.

She gasped, grinding against me. Her legs tightened, and she released a throaty chuckle. "So, am I a bad girl?" she asked, teasing my mouth with hers.

"No, baby. You're a good girl."

Still, she withheld her kiss.

"I want to be a good girl for you." She rocked her hips.

My balls tightened. "Lift your arms, Dani."

Releasing my hair, she lifted her arms, and I ran my nose over her smooth collarbone, drawing her scent into my lungs. I slid her dress off, putting my mouth on her exposed skin. She worked on my shirt, and I helped. Feeling her smooth curves against my front was like pressing into heaven. Her hands and lips slid over me until finally, her mouth met mine. She never paused rocking, her speed picking up.

My knuckles pressed into her as I worked on my zipper. "Tell me you're on birth control," I demanded. Frankly, I didn't care what her answer was. I would have her either way.

"Yes," she gasped.

"Good girl." I bit her bottom lip, sucking it between my teeth. Pulling myself free of my pants, she lifted, her perfect thighs gripping me, angling.

I wanted to devour her, try her from every imaginable position. My tip found her slick and swollen. "So fucking wet for me." I grasped her waist, preventing her from her needy drive down on me. My lower back tensed. "My eyes, Dani."

She opened her eyes, slightly dazed. Every hot, tight inch of her settled around me as I allowed her to descend. She whimpered into my mouth while holding my gaze.

"*Fuck*. You are perfect, baby."

Her body trembled, and she shifted, allowing me deeper. Deeper, but not enough, and too much at the same time.

We stayed locked like that for several heartbeats, a tether forming in that most intimate moment. With each exhale, she released a soft "ah."

"You are perfect," I repeated. Saw the doubt flash in those too-bright eyes. "Beautiful." I lifted her and pulled her back down. Up and down. Slowly. Steadily. In sync with our breathing.

She blinked but still held my gaze. "You're fucking perfect, Orion. Strong. Sexy. Gorgeous."

The way her voice quavered made the moths in my stomach tipsy. I quirked a brow. "Aren't sexy and gorgeous redundant?"

"No." She picked up the pace and continued whispering praises. "I see you. I feel you. So deep. Fuck. Orion. So. Deep. Oh."

My lower abdominal muscles tensed. I wouldn't last much longer. By the way her body tightened, she wouldn't either.

"Come for me, Dani."

She cried out right before my orgasm slammed into me, a rush of power and bliss with each dynamic pulse.

We collapsed into each other, and I held her like I would a lifeline, even though I felt like I was falling. And what a beautiful fucking drop.

TWENTY-SIX

DANI

After I visited the bathroom, I opened the window. The ocean breeze would be a nice welcome come morning, but for now, I only wanted the sound of the waves to help smother the chaotic yammering of my thoughts.

Orion lay like a Greek god in my bed, an arm behind his head, the other resting on his thigh. The bed sheet draped across him, his other leg pulled up, knee in the air. On my approach, he let his knee fall to the side.

I tugged the sheet away and looked at him. Felt his gaze burn into me. A few long scars decorated his beautiful form. Several tribal tattoos graced his shoulders.

"What do they represent?"

"Come here," he commended in a gruff voice. "Crawl. Slow."

I narrowed my eyes and crawled as if I was sneaking up on my prey. Slowly. Deliberately. When my arms and legs straddled his body, I leaned down and licked his neck before biting down. My reward was his soft groan.

"I asked you a question, Marine." I sat up, hands on my thighs, my center on his taut stomach, and stared down at him with as much authority as a naked woman in heat might look.

My path led straight past Go to wrecked without redemption.

His smile alone caused a cascading reaction in my bones. The flutter of excitement, the building warmth, my every sense homed in on him. The way his calloused hands brushed lightly over my flesh. The rise and fall of his chest. I eased back down his form until I sat on his thighs, then motioned for him to sit up.

"You think by flashing your dimples you can get me to do anything?" He sat up, his abdominal muscles contracting from the movement.

Physically, his drool-worthy body was hard not to ogle or touch. While not an enormous beast of a man, he had broad shoulders and powerful arms. I ran my hands over his skin, tracing the lines of his muscles, the powerful V of his lower abdomen. I considered every inch of his perfectly imperfect skin, marred by a few scars. The sheer power of his body and the way he seemed to fill the room with his masculinity mesmerized me.

Pulling my gaze away from his torso, I met his fervent gaze that intensified the heat pooling low in my body. Face to face, I palmed his right forearm and pulled it between us. "This one first."

With a fingertip, I traced the ouroboros dream catcher. Inked in black, the extraordinary combination suggested significance for the man in my bed. The ouroboros snake was incredibly detailed for a tattoo.

"The dreamcatcher symbolizes protection from negative thoughts and dreams. My buddy had an ouroboros that I really liked, and he suggested combining it with the dream catcher."

"Life. Death. Rebirth."

"Yeah." His chest rumbled low, almost like the growl of a wolf. He took my hand in his and traced the feathers. "The feathers represent strength and bravery. Reminders to never give up. The butterfly," he tapped the tiny insect in flight next to the center feather. "Stands for transformation."

I inspected the delicate image. "Are those stars on its wings?"

"Beautiful and perceptive." He tapped the tip of my nose.

"Flattery will get you many things."

He nuzzled his face into my chest, his nose rubbing my sternum. His breath tickled, but this was a learning moment, so I cupped his cheeks and drew his face to mine. After a soft kiss, I said, "Other side."

He nipped my lower lip, and I felt the sensation in my groin. "Yes, ma'am."

On his right upper arm was inked a gorgeous bison bull head with a shield painted over one eye. On the opposite side of the face on the nose, a partially exposed skull showed. Geometric lines and circles radiated outward from the image. "Strength?" I guessed. "Or an NDSU fan?"

He rewarded me with a bright smile. "Yes, and yes. Also endurance. Survival."

Sadness touched the dip in between his eyebrows and lessened the curve of his lips. While he had one more tattoo to share, I decided at that moment we needed to celebrate both of our survival stories.

Gliding my hands over his shoulders, I marveled at his muscles. The strength they showed. The scar beneath his left collarbone.

I leaned in and kissed it. His hands weaved into my loose hair, gripping and tugging my face to his. I gave in to the sensations, to feel him in every way possible. His grip on my hair relaxed and I leaned my head back and closed my eyes, losing myself to the feel of his hands exploring my body, his mouth my skin.

His fingers lingered on my throat, feather-light, before they made their way up to cradle my face. His other hand slid over the mound of my breast and down my rib cage. Goosebumps followed in their wake. He reached around my back and pressed me closer to him. I felt him draw out a groan before his lips met mine in an onslaught of hunger. As he deepened the kiss, he explored every crevice of my mouth with increasing ferocity. I felt each swipe of his tongue as a burst of heat between my legs. His hands gripped my waist, and I rose on my knees and he followed, our bodies entwined in a passionate embrace. His fingertips blaze a trail along my curves and spine, setting off sparks of pleasure throughout my body.

I broke off the kiss and buried my face in his soft hair, inhaling the scent of his shampoo. Orion whispered my name, the hot air curling into the hollow at the base of my neck. He ran his nose over my flesh, and I pressed my body against his with each movement. His hands massaged my curves while his fingers traced circles on my skin, sending little electric shocks that surged through me.

His hands were solid, hard, and unyielding. Orion didn't just run his hands over my skin. He ran them across my skin as if he were marking me as his territory. He sent me higher until I felt like I might drift too far from Earth and never want to return.

His lips caressed my neck, and I tilted my head to the side, allowing him to explore every inch of my skin with his teeth and tongue. He brought one hand to my breast, his wet fingertips grazing over one nipple while his mouth closed over the other. His hot tongue flicked and teased before he sucked hard. I felt euphoria in my toes. His fingers found their way inside me, his strokes urgent. I could feel my climax building, my body coiling tightly with each stroke.

"Dani," he whispered my name with a reverence and longing that drew a sob from my lips.

"So close," I whimpered.

I felt the rumble of his laughter as the initial sparks of an orgasm hit and my hips bucked against his hand.

"Shit." I drew out the word, as I dropped my head back, my hair grazing my ass.

He bit down on my other nipple, the sharp pain sending off another shower of sparks in my core, and I squealed.

"So responsive. Do you want to get off on my fingers or my dick?"

He slid his fingers out of me, with a pressure that damn near undid me. My mind could only focus on the loss of him. My needy body jolted with each touch of skin or hint of breath. I whimpered, unable to articulate my need.

"I got you, baby."

His fingers ghosted up over my throat, then moved to cup my face, and before I knew it, his lips were on mine once more, gentle and passionate. I parted my lips, and he deepened the kiss. The wiry hair of his chest tickled my belly, my breasts. My entire being simmered, one degree away from roiling out of control. His hands traveled lower, sliding along my curves until they reached my waist, guiding my way.

He twisted, turning to lay me on my back. The sheets were warm on my skin. I clutched at them as he settled between my legs. Beside my head, he braced himself on his elbow.

He lifted his body away from me and looked between us. I glanced down to see what he saw but got caught up in the movement of his free hand. He smoothed his palm over my skin, triggering a rush of tiny explosions within me. I stretched and arched into him.

He gripped my hip, and I felt his cock at my slick entrance, my walls aching with the need for him to bury his length inside me again and again. To destroy me. Shatter me into a million pieces, then draw me back together. Ravage and ruin me before breathing new life into me.

As if reading my mind, he did exactly that. Our bodies came together in perfect harmony. He flexed and pumped, my legs wrapped around his taught thighs. I met him, thrust for thrust, rocking as my orgasm washed over me, the contractions so intense stars flashed across my vision. The spasms continued as Orion jerked and panted lost in his own throes. He punctuated each pulse inside me with a grunt next to my ear, which resulted in another round of tightening and spiraling pleasure in my belly. I never wanted it to end.

Giddy laughter escaped me as I jockeyed beneath him, grinding and extending my rapture. His grip tightened, and he sucked in a breath. My lips found his, and I stilled my hip action, my chest heaving for air.

"Fuck, Dani."

"Sorry," I began. He was too sensitive. I took too much.

He tugged my waist, pumping himself inside me once more, and I cried out.

"Stop. Saying. You're sorry." He panted and rested his forehead on mine. "Although I need a minute." He chuckled.

I hugged him close, feeling his heart race. My heart thundered, and I wondered what this was between us. He gave, allowed me to take. Made me experience pleasure that was so good it pained me. And I wanted more. When would reality set in, or was this what reality was like with Orion?

He collapsed against me, my body trembling as I wrapped my arms around him. Savoring the sensations of that intimate moment, I felt serene and safe in his arms.

TWENTY-SEVEN

ORION

The next morning, we got out of bed long enough to feed the animals and give them attention. Feed ourselves. Shower. The last bit was my favorite part.

As we scrubbed each other, Dani said, "I realize we've only met, and, um, well..."

She stood beneath the showerhead holding a sudsy loofah. The steady heat of a spring rain inside a volcano cocooned us.

"What I mean is, you're clean, right? I am. Haven't been with anyone else besides my ex."

"And you're thinking that since I'm a Marine, I'm what? Promiscuous?"

I teased, but she didn't look like she picked up on it, if I correctly gauged the slight frown that tugged at her kissable lips.

I placed a finger beneath her chin and tilted her head up. "I'm healthy. Promise. I may not enjoy talking about myself..."

"Or talking period..."

I laughed because, hey; she wasn't wrong.

"Turn around and let me wash your hair. I have to fess up to something and I'd rather not face you when I do it," she said.

Obliging, I did as she asked.

"This eagle is amazing," she said, spraying her hands out over my shoulder blades.

"That's a Chippewa symbol."

"It's a beaut." She cleared her throat. "I read a background check on you. Before I invited you to stay."

"Smart girl." I was curious if it mentioned my medical discharge. Then I realized she said read, not ran.

Her fingers dug into my scalp, kneading it like bread dough. Both stimulating and soothing, I knew how Thor felt when I scratched the "sweet spot." I groaned, dropping my head back. She continued her massage.

"Guess what I found?"

"Hmmm. Nothing?"

"Nothing. Squeaky clean."

So, a medical discharge did not show up on a civilian background check.

"I also called the clinic you took Thor to get his rabies."

I turned, and her hands fell away from my head. "Checking on my story."

She gave a shy smile before her eyebrows furrowed and the corners of her mouth dipped. "I hope you don't mind."

"I don't. To be honest, I think I'd mind more if you hadn't."

The water streamed over her skin and dripped from her erect nipples. Her dark hair molded to her head and draped heavily across her shoulders. Steam collected in droplets on her thick, dark eyelashes. She was exquisite.

She deserved far better than me. The thought struck me that if given the chance, I would do anything to deserve her. For a guy who liked to keep people at arm's length, the idea felt raw. Peculiar. I decided to give her a piece of me. "A few months ago, I received a medical discharge from the Marines. My plan had been to retire, but I came up nearly eight years short."

"I'm sorry, Orion."

I pressed my forehead to hers, and she wrapped her arms around me.

"Me, too. I've been trying to figure out what to do next. Been waylaid by the reasons for my discharge."

She remained quiet, softly skating her hands up and down the planes of my back.

"I have anxiety, depression, and PTSD."

"And the injury to your calf."

I gazed at her. Smart and eidetic?

"So, are you upset with me?" she asked.

"About checking up on me? No. I'm impressed."

"Really?"

"Yeah. Tells me you're very interested in me." I kissed her nose.

"Or just making sure I wasn't taking in a psycho, although the jury is still out..."

She squirmed as I grabbed her ass and lifted her.

"Hey." She laughed and centered herself, wrapping her legs around my waist.

I was ready for her again.

"Otherwise, you have a clean bill of health?"

Back to that.

"Hop down," I ordered.

She mock-saluted me. "Yes, sir."

"Hmm. I like the submission. Yes. No STDs. Also..." Drawing her into my arms, I told her a story. "Once upon a time," I began, using her words from the night before.

Tilting her head back, she gazed at me with her big green eyes. She rested her chin on my sternum and gave me a gentle smile, her dimple appearing.

I leaned forward and kissed it before going on.

"There was a cocky young man who loved sports. We'll call him the Greek Hunter."

She chuckled, and the press of her breasts to my chest momentarily distracted me. So, too, did the shape of her hands as they stroked my lower back and ass. Would I ever get enough of her?

"One day, while playing basketball with his brothers and a few friends, the Greek Hunter went for a shot. A nearby player lost his balance when the person he was guarding ran into him. As the Greek Hunter came down from taking his shot, his teammate fell into him. They went down in a tangle, the Greek Hunter first on the pavement.

"Unfortunately, the Greek Hunter had a pencil in his pocket. Murphy's Law came into play that hot summer day. The pencil stabbed through the topmost of the man's scrotum."

Dani's arms tightened around me. "Oh, no."

"Yeah. At a young age, I had a sudden, involuntary vasectomy. Very embarrassing for me. My dad insisted it was not a bad thing. 'No girl will ever falsely accuse you of getting her pregnant.'" I made my low voice change to a gruff pitch in a poor imitation of my father. I cleared my throat before continuing. "Side story, my uncle had gotten his girlfriend pregnant in high school, but when the baby was born, he couldn't shake the feeling it wasn't his. And a secret paternity test proved it wasn't, but he stayed with her and raised my cousin as his own kid.

"Anyway. I've worn a rubber every time. Since my last tour, I haven't been interested in much of anything." I tugged on her hair so her head tipped back and she looked me in the eye. She didn't need to hear about my escapades. "Until my sweet ass ran into you."

"Mmmm. And such a sweet ass it is. So sweet you made me break my rules."

She kissed me with a vehemence reserved for the starving being offered a buffet. Before my thoughts focused on my carnal urges, I contemplated my infertility. Honestly, I had never really considered kids. Never had a long-term relationship, not with my long stretches of deployment. I didn't want ties, not until I was older. My buddies made fun of me. "Just wait. The right girl will come along and tie you the fuck down."

I didn't want ties. There was a world to explore, and looking back, a simmering pot of unaddressed anxiety and depression that worked against me in relationships.

Dani brought out thoughts and feelings occasionally more uncomfortable than reliving my past, so instead, I focused on her body.

Later in the afternoon, we set out to wrestling practice.

"My brother Elliot is the assistant coach."

"Let me guess. He wrestled. Eamon wrestled. You wrestled. And your nephews and niece wrestle?"

"Uh-huh. Walker and Genesis are Elliot's kids. Senior and junior. Wynn is an eighth grader."

"Got it."

She grabbed my hand and tugged me close as we walked across the pavement to the school. "Do you really?"

"Yes. I should be terrified of your family. A doctor, lawyer, wrestlers, veterinarian. All scary folks."

"Did I mention I can legally castrate seven species of animals?"

"Ain't that the biggest turn-on?" And it was, the thought of her handling my nuts, anyway. Thank God she didn't have a license to *remove* mine. After kissing her thoroughly, we headed into the school.

It felt good to go through warm-ups. I hadn't run that morning, not that I didn't take a morning off from time to time. Dani had put me through several bouts of cardio, so I figured I was good.

Wrestling practice brought back fond memories. It was a challenging sport. You handled your own matches, yet your team carried your wins and losses. Wrestlers spent hours together. Stayed overnight in hotels for early weigh-ins, unlike other sports. I could be biased, but I thought it was the best sport.

As the coaches oversaw matches and drills, Dani and I walked among the group, offering help. Together, we showed improvements in the techniques. They used me as a dummy more often than not. One young girl was struggling with her stance, and after I worked with her on her foot grip and suggested running workouts on her toes, she stopped getting pushed off balance.

With that one small thing, the rush of accomplishment was incredible.

Dani... let me tell you. Watching her wrestle her brother, Eamon, for fun at the end before burnout was, dare I say, breathtaking. Of course, I rooted for Dani. She was the same height as her brother, close to the same weight, too. And their skill... she had held back in telling me about wrestling. Both of them. You could tell they wrestled together often and knew each other's signature moves. Dani sprawled, and they tied up. Restarted. Elliot whispered to Eamon before they started another round.

Eamon threw a headlock, and I figured it was over. But Dani stepped into him, her shoulder sliding across his chest as she wrapped her arms around his waist and lifted.

She dropped them both to the ground and was on his back, grabbing at his foot.

He pulled himself onto his hands and knees like a turtle. Dani threw her chest over his side and moved her lower body across his to the side of her leg hold. In seconds, she had him rolled over onto his spine.

One coach called it, and Dani and Eamon instructed the high schooler on the succession of moves in slow motion. The headlock escape into a cradle.

Later, she and I did burnout at the back of the room, both of us smiling even though I certainly wanted to puke.

This woman kept getting higher and higher on the point scale.

TWENTY-EIGHT

ORION

Elliot and Eamon walked out to the parking lot with us, Elliot sharing news that the work on my Bronco was nearly done.

"Some paint work to go, then you should be ready to head out."

I glanced at Dani. Her face remained flushed but impassive.

"Great, thanks, man."

Eamon, chattier than the other two, said, "You're staying with Dani?" He crossed his arms and stared me down. Younger and lighter than Elliot, Eamon also had short, stylized hair.

"Yes, sir. The cottage is perfect."

Elliot flicked his eyes to Dani. "Can't beat the ocean view, am I right?"

"Where you from, Orion?" Eamon asked.

"Camp Pendleton."

"Right. But where's home for you?"

I slipped my hands behind my back in a stand-easy pose. "Currently, your sister's cottage."

"What are your future plans?" Eamon started, but Dani grabbed my arm.

"Come on. This is not a hazing. Orion isn't staying long. No need for twenty questions." She rolled her eyes. A pretty pink blush crept up her throat and bloomed onto her cheeks.

Her phone rang, and she stepped away, answering without looking. "Hello?"

Elliot stepped close and murmured loud enough for me and Eamon to hear. "Look. I feel pretty confident you are a good dude. It's a gut feeling. I hope I'm not wrong. We love our sister, so I'm gonna say this once. Don't fuck with her."

"Be better if you leave soon. Before she gets too attached," Eamon added. "We made the mistake with Dickface. We don't want a repeat of him in her life."

"You're not a parrot she can mend and give a home. We will make your life hell if you hurt her."

Gee, thanks, Ell. Suddenly, my life was cast in all shades of awkwardness as I stood there, uncertain what to say.

Dani and I better have a conversation. If her brothers thought we were an item, did she? Although hadn't I already pictured a future with her?

"No, sir." I felt like I was in high school getting ready to take her to prom. "She is extraordinary and I—" I didn't have time to finish.

Eamon's gaze trained on Dani as he said, "Dani? Hey, what's wrong?"

She stood a few feet away, her brows furrowed. "Um. Nothing?"

Elliot approached with Eamon on his heels. They looked at her phone.

"That's a Wisconsin area code," Eamon said. "Again."

Again? Wisconsin rang a bell. Wasn't that where she lived before when she was married?

"It's probably nothing," Dani said, pinching her bottom lip between her fingers.

"Oh yeah? Who was it?" Elliot asked.

Dani crossed her arms, squeezing her biceps. Goosebumps broke over her skin. "There wasn't anyone on the other end."

Eamon said, "Give me your phone, sis. Please."

"Since you asked so nicely," Dani quipped, although her face pinched in worry.

On his personal phone, he dialed the number while on speaker. A man answered. "Hello?"

"Who the fuck is this?" Eamon began, but Dani had already reached over and hit the end button.

Her face had paled and as her brothers stared at her with identical *what the fuck* looks, she cleared her throat. "Sorry. It sounded like, well. Someone I knew."

Elliot straightened. "Dickface?"

Dani leaned against her Mini and crossed her arms. Her eyes misted and her fingers blanched from the tightened grip. In fact, all color drained from her sun-kissed face.

I stepped to her side, unsure of what to do. I suspected I knew who they referred to, but never assume, right?

"Dani, the camera and alarms are working on the property, right?"

"Um, yeah. Well, not the cameras on the back of the house. I don't like video surveillance of my evenings."

"Tough shit. Get them turned on. You." Eamon pointed to me. "Stay with Dani in the main house until we figure this out."

Seeming to shake herself out of whatever storm brewed within, she gave a hollow laugh. "It's fine, guys. He can't get to me. It was probably a wrong number."

Her phone rang again. She glanced at the screen, then ignored it. Her message notification dinged.

The phone ringing spiked my anxiety. I couldn't imagine what it was doing to Dani. When I could, I gently took Dani's phone and shut it off.

"She's off work for the weekend. No need for your phone, right Dani?" I asked her.

"I just had my number changed. Fuck." Dani lifted her face, tears falling. "Take me home."

Eamon and Elliot both hugged her, whispering to her during their turn. She nodded, eyes downcast. When she was settled and seat belted, Elliot placed a hand on my shoulder. The moths in my stomach beat against their confines and the back of my neck prickled with dread.

Elliot explained they would notify their parents. "Our mom can check with the PI. Make sure Dickface is where he should be."

"Dani told me a little about him." Would they share more? Turns out they were willing.

"Did she tell you she was married to a controlling narcissist? That after Darius Dickface Taylor psychologically abused her, he moved on to beating the shit out of her? Raped her because she owed him it as his wife?"

The moths settled, and a viper rose in their place. My instinct to protect calmed the anxiety and gave me purpose. I straightened and stared back at them, a vigorous pulse hammering away in my ears. The visceral feeling I had when she shared her story the other night, barely scraping the surface of her and her ex's relationship, had been dead on.

Elliot continued, "No. She wouldn't tell you those things, or that he killed her dog after she filed for divorce."

God damn him. My body grew rigid, and I felt my muscles tighten. Although I just worked out for two and a half hours, my adrenaline spiked, and I felt ready to hand out a beatdown. Fisting my hands, I said, "Not in those terms." My short fingernails dug into my palms.

"Darius fuckin' Taylor. Dani never wanted to press charges, just wanted to be done with him. Where they were married, well, the state doesn't give two shits about who hurt who. They split everything down the middle."

Eamon took over the narrative. "Problem is, he knows about our parents' many homes. Dad offered to buy Dani one, but she declined. She loves the ocean house so much."

I made sure they both had my number, checked to make sure my phone notification volume was off mute, and then drove Dani home.

TWENTY-NINE

DANI

My mind raced on the drive home. Why? Why did Darius feel the need to harass me? Did he not have a life to move on with? Could he not find someone else to bother? Was I that much of a thorn in his side that he had to destroy me entirely?

I wanted to curl up and cry. My world felt tilted, a slippery slope that I traveled down at lightning speed, making it difficult to jump off. Even if I could, how would I land? On my feet like Bunnie or splat like a bug on a windshield?

The beautiful distraction beside me radiated anger and hostility. A small part of me realized the anger wasn't directed at me, yet I held responsible for his emotional state. And suddenly I knew it would not end well with Orion. I wanted to scream. He would realize soon that he needed no part of the madness of my life. Already my heart felt fractured, the ache of a coming heartbreak edging into my life.

Overwhelming disbelief, horror, and fear clawed their way up my throat.

"Stop. Stop right now." My voice sounded hollow to my ringing ears.

Orion pulled over, and I tumbled out, retching onto the dry earth, my lower half hung up in the car.

Then he was there, helping me out of the uncomfortable position. Wiping my hair off my sweaty face. Placing a moist towelette in my hands while dabbing my skin.

He was an angel taken in by a demon's bride. Ex-bride. Did that make me a demon by association? Maybe I was the greatest monster he ever faced, especially since I somehow attracted Darius back into my life.

"I'm so sorry." My incoherent sobs were pathetic in my ears. I shouldn't be apologetic. I should tell him to leave.

But I selfishly needed him to chase away my boogeyman, at least for now.

He would realize soon enough I'm too much trouble, my past too dark to allow him any light.

ORION

Back at Dani's I opened the door to the kennel, and Thor shot out like a cannon, barreling straight toward her. The connection between them was unmistakable, and it made something inside me wistful. I wished I had the same ability to let my guard down around her as Thor did. He had an easy way of connecting with people that I could only dream of having, and I wanted her to be just as open with me. Even though I knew it wasn't fair to begrudge him, I couldn't deny my envy of the little guy, especially as Dani lay on the floor and played with him.

After her sick episode, she grew quiet, her arms crossed as if holding herself together.

Reining in my anger and fear over her ex had been difficult. Protecting someone against a psychological threat... how does one do that? And would Darius follow up physically? The same helplessness I shared with her brothers settled like a heavy weight in my gut.

I wanted to distract her. Comfort her. Make her feel safe. I wanted to kill the guy. The latter would certainly resolve the former, but place me far away from her, and that harsh, terrifying reality startled me.

As dusk fell, we ventured along the beach. The night sky descended like a blanket; the full moon illuminated the waves serenely lapping against the shore. There was no hum from the road here. It was just me and her in this alternate realm, the stillness of the night broken only by the occasional skitter of Thor across the sand.

We walked alongside the shoreline in silence, Thor bounding ahead. The peace of the moment was strangely comforting, and despite my apprehension, I felt my body relax as if I had taken a Xanax.

I glanced over at Dani, who seemed lost in her own thoughts. She had been unusually quiet since we'd arrived. I wanted to ask her how she was, but at the same time, I was afraid of what she might say.

Finally, gathering my courage, I said softly, "Dani... do you want to talk about it?"

Placing an arm around her shoulder, I pulled her close in a gentle embrace and whispered words of comfort. She stepped into me and leaned her head against my chest, her breathing slow and even.

"I'm sorry to drag you into my drama," she said, a hint of weariness in her voice.

I tightened my arms around her. "You didn't drag me. Do you want to talk?"

She shook her head, then tilted it back to look up at me.

"No? Hmm. Then, how about sex on the beach?"

That startled a brittle laugh from her. "That would be awesome if we could manage not to get sand in every nook and cranny. And if the water was remotely warm."

"Now who's the Negative Nancy?" I teased.

"Obviously you are. I'm being a realist," she retorted before melting into me as I kissed her.

Thor jumped up to join us, begging to be included in the group hug.

Giving in, I rearranged my sweats as I picked him up. He rewarded me with slow licks across my whiskered face. Dani stiffly sat on the sand, her body coiled around her knees like a steel spring.

I dropped beside her, and Thor weaseled his way onto her lap. He, like the ocean, was better than medication. We stayed like that, quiet for an hour until darkness had fully settled. Above, the stars became bright pinpoints. The sand was soft beneath my bare feet, and the warm salty sea air offset the cool chill of the beach.

My phone buzzed in my pocket. "It's Elliot."

"Oh. I left my phone at the house," Dani said.

I answered, "Hello, Elliot. Got you on speaker."

"Hey guys. News for you. Darius is still in Wisconsin. Mom filed an updated restraining order to include every location where she and Dad own homes. There is no sign on social media or his internet browsing that he knows where you are."

Interesting. How did one get another's internet browsing data? Legally?

I asked, "How did he get her phone number?"

Elliot paused. "Not sure."

After that, the more I attempted to draw Dani from the shell she had fortified around herself, the more she withdrew.

Back at the house, I fixed sandwiches for us. Dani nibbled on hers.

She let the parrots into the house. Their outdoor enclosure opened into a spare room with a TV and couch for humans, an enormous cat emporium for Bunnie, and multiple swings and perches for the birds.

Snow settled on her back in my arms, and I cradled her like a baby. Timsy sat on a perch behind the couch next to Dani. Fleur parked her large body in the far corner and called out, making the room sound like a jungle.

We watched Dani's favorite movie, *The Man from Snowy River*, then returned the birds to their outdoor enclosure. Timsy called out for Jess as we slipped off to bed.

Dani had been unnervingly solemn, and Timsy's jest failed to jog her out of it. Grief over her own worries plagued me like pregnant storm clouds blocking my sunshine.

I eventually herded her to the bedroom. Unsure what to do, I kept silent, guarding her like an angry demon, with hellfire burning through my veins. She curled into me in her king-sized bed. I had opened the window to hear the ocean, and a cool breeze swayed the lacy curtains. Normally comfortable to not talk, the silence bore down on me with suffocating gravity.

I pulled the sheet up over us and she nestled into me, her head tucked beneath my chin, and whispered, "This is called a military cover-up."

I felt her soft chuckle and was elated to have gotten through her dreariness with my humor. "When I first met you—"

"You mean when I ran my vehicle into yours?"

"Eh, semantics. I was pissed because I thought you'd been drinking. And then I was pissed because you were driving under the influence of the Sandman."

She rewarded me with a small smile. "Sounds like you're just a pissy guy." Her sad eyes seemed to glow in the dim.

"But wait, there's more." My dry chuckle earned a greater curve in her beautiful mouth. I brushed my thumb over the rise and fall of her shoulder. "Then you irritated the hell outta me because of your sunshiny smile and look-on-the-bright-side kind of personality. I eventually recognized it wasn't an act. You truly were trying your hardest to find the bright spot in everyday life. You know how easy it is to slip into the shadows and get lost in the darkness."

She had slid out of the light effortlessly earlier that evening.

Her smile faltered. "And you, Orion... You prefer the shadows."

Her words did not cut like they once would have, the truth sometimes having a sharp bite. "I can find a happy place, but more often, I have to make one. And it is easier to not put forth the effort." I tugged the comforter over us, enveloping us in a muffled cave of fabric, the contours of her body areas I wished to explore further until I knew them by heart. For now, snuggled in. "I'd gladly explore the shadows with you, Dani."

Her palm cupped my jaw as she ran her thumb over my cheek. She hummed once and lifted her head. I slid my arm behind her and she settled into me, her hand stroking my stubble. When she moved to my hair and began a slow, rhythmic, one-handed head massage, I closed the distance between us.

Her faint perfume, the tantalizing mix of sweet, comforting, and arousing, bloomed up. Combined with our joint, slightly sweaty bodies, and recent sexual endeavors, the aroma... if I could bottle it, I would wear it every day.

I caught her lips in a slow, explorative kiss.

Her other hand moved between us and rested on my chest, her fingers threading through my limited chest hair. Meanwhile, I grazed the back of my free hand over her curves, my other hand resting lightly on her shoulder.

We took our time. Our kisses fluctuated from deep, thorough kisses to light, feathery touches. Succulent draws and nibbles on her lips. On mine. I drew her leg over my waist, my fingers drawing provocative patterns on her thigh and ass.

I did not push for more. Rather, I relished her sweetness. The intimacy was far deeper than sex, and so addicting that I didn't want to stop. I rode it out as long as I could until I sensed her ragged edges fusing with my jagged ones. It both terrified and delighted me. But that was something to think about another time.

Her fingernails dug into my scalp. Not painfully. Scouring. Her hips started moving, rubbing her soaked center along my throbbing erection. Unconsciously, I had been working her closer.

"Tell me you're okay with this. That I'm not just a distraction." I paused. No. Too fast. I would be leaving. Would have to leave. "Or that you want a distraction. I'll distract you repeatedly."

She raised a delicate brow, and her dimple appeared. "Repeatedly? I love the sound of that." Her voice took on an ethereal, husky tone.

I rolled onto my back, and she moved along with me effortlessly and straddled me. She caged my head with her arms and snaked herself up the length of my dick until my tip pressed right into the door to heaven.

"Thank you," she said between peppering kisses along my throat and collarbone.

"For what?" My balls jacked up as she slipped her slick, tight self over my cock. My vision tunneled and when I felt her walls contract, a fucking explosion of colors happened within our blanket cave.

She paused, her words breathless. "For not treating me with pity. Or like I was some fragile thing." She lifted and rocked slowly, working just inside her.

"*Fuck*, baby. What are you doing to me?"

"Distracting you."

The moths fluttered, sourly, in my stomach as I realized she took what I meant to heart. Distraction. Rather than dissecting the rising emotions, I focused on her. Her perfect fit. The feel of her flesh bending and pushing into mine.

I'll give her distraction in the form of a total loss of control. "Come up here, baby, and straddle my face."

Her eyes widened, and she stilled her lower body. Panting slightly, she stared down at me.

"I've never done that." Her words came out halting and quiet.

Never received oral sex or never face-fucked. She was what, in her thirties? Should I have asked? I'll be honest. I'm not great at discussions. There was so much I didn't know about her, but now was not the time to learn anything more than how many times I could make her scream my name as she came.

I pushed up on my elbows where she hovered above me, uncertainty flashing in her eyes. I didn't want to push her into anything she was uncomfortable with. "Do you want to stay in our cave?" I whispered against her lips.

She nodded. "There's comfort in the darkness."

"What do you mean?" I thought I might understand but wanted to hear her speak.

"Sometimes, I cannot escape the dark void that builds inside me. Immersing myself in the dark... it's like an embrace."

She had become solemn. "Then lie down on your back for me, Dani." There's comfort in the darkness, that I knew. "Do you find yourself searching for dark places?"

Dani shrugged and didn't meet my gaze. Pointedly looking everywhere but me.

"We both have plenty of monsters. How about I be your darkness, give you some needed comfort?"

"Like the kind given when you're between my legs?"

Yes, and more. I knew she was uncomfortable with my exhibition request, so deciding instead to give her time to consider it, I crawled up and lay beside her, pulling her back into my chest. One hand flat on the slight swell of her belly, the other palming her shoulder as my arm draped around her neck.

Suddenly wanting only to hold her tightly to me, I said, "I find it easier to say things in the shadows. Whisper secrets. The light makes some things seem too ugly or depraved."

She countered, "The light brings out beauty, colors, and vibrant motion."

I hummed into her hair as I stroked her side. She shivered. "I'm angry. Not sad. Angry. He stole my youth."

Silent, I listened as she poured out her frustrations. That she even as he made her life hell, she prayed for a child. "So dumb of me to want to bring a new life into that hellscape. But my biological clock kept ticking. Still is ticking. I'm getting old. Sorry," she exhaled.

"Don't be sorry, Dani. And you are not old." I tightened my grip around her. My groin responded to the friction.

"This is not a plea for you to knock me up." Her chest rumbled with a chuckle.

"That would be an impossibility," I reminded her, suddenly sad for that fact.

We stayed that way, lost in our thoughts, we drifted in and out of sleep until she nudged me with her hip. Pulling my hand up to her face, she kissed my palm. "Okay, Orion. What would you like me to do?"

Sleep muddled, it took me a moment to remember where I was. "Me."

She laughed. "Yes. That is a given. What do you want me to do?"

I moved, rolling her to her back as I came to rest in the cradle of her legs.

Her legs tensed against my shoulders as I moved to my knees. I pressed her legs down into the mattress and rearranged the bed sheet, so it tented over us. For several moments, I looked at every glorious inch of her visible in the dusky, dim light that filtered through the sheet. She, the goddess, and me, her acolyte.

"I'm not good with words, Dani."

"But you are with your tongue?" Her tease sounded flat. Humor during times of discomfort.

I needed her to know she could relax. That I would take care of her.

The realization then that I wanted to take care of her didn't shock me as much as it should have.

"Shall we find out?" I gave her a wink and a gentle squeeze on the insides of her soft thighs.

She rolled her bottom lip into her mouth and bit down, her expression slowly relaxing.

"You are gorgeous, Dani. I need you to know I think that. Gorgeous. Sexy. Funny. Incredibly smart."

"How sincere should I take your words when you're between my legs looking at me like I'm your last meal?"

"Very, very sincere."

Then I slid down the length of her body and showed how sincere I was.

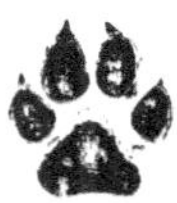

We took a break around midnight and broke open a quart of salted caramel and vanilla ice cream. She seemed embarrassed to be living in her parents' home. Correction. It was to be her home soon. Besides, with their jobs, they had accumulated several. They didn't need the beach house. "What is it you told me? It doesn't make you weak to accept help from others?"

She lightly punched my arm. Once again, her smile dazzled me. I leaned over and kissed her, licking the salted sweetness from her mouth. It was so easy, losing myself in her.

Two more nights of intimacy showed me how much I craved her.

We would instinctively finish one another's sentences as if we were one of those Disney couples. But even as my chest felt like it was about to burst with joy, images of bodies in tatters and mutilated faces jolted me from my current reality.

Even as Dani comforted me, I knew that my connection with her was as fleeting as the moment. I tried to distract her from her own nightmares, but I felt guilty indulging in our physical intimacy. How long could this continue before it all fell apart?

And her own nightmares... would she open up more to me? Could I help her fight her demons?

THIRTY-ONE

DANI

Military cover-up. I rolled my eyes even as the heat rolled off him within the stuffy cave he had built us. I didn't want to move because that would mean returning to reality.

Staying like this made me feel safe. Like it was only the two of us.

Something wiggled against my foot. Thor scratching his something. Not the two of us, then.

I relished the heat because it meant he was still here.

It was not the time to wonder how long Orion would stick around.

Weight pushed me into the mattress. It was hard to breathe, and I gasped in pain as something clutched my hip. Orion groaned and gasped, the sounds not erotic but devastating, and overwhelming me with grief that was not my own.

He clung desperately to my thighs; his upper body draped over me like a desperate man clinging to a surfboard upon a violent sea. I knew he lived in a nightmare, and I didn't want to wake him suddenly. Better to ease him out of it.

His smooth skin glistened with perspiration. Eyelids heavy. Muscles taut. His breathing labored.

I hummed and threaded my fingers through his short hair and alternated between kneading his scalp and scraping my nails against his skin.

His body gradually relaxed and the thudding of his heart decelerated.

With gentle encouragement, I urged him to lift his head and when he did, his deep navy-blue eyes met mine with a look that pierced through me.

"Hey," I whispered, smiling up at him.

Orion glanced around the room before looking back down at me, confusion etching onto his face as he realized where we were. He released his grip on my thighs and stretched out his sore hands before dropping his forehead against my sternum. Continuing my humming, I intertwined my fingers into his dark hair, grateful to have been there for him in such an intimate moment.

"God, you are beautiful," he murmured, his hard length pressing against my calf. He shifted, settling between my legs.

"I didn't realize you thought God was attractive," I teased before he took a nipple into his mouth and bit down hard enough that I gasped. The sensation coursed through me like liquid fire.

He chuckled lightly in between my breasts, his breath fanning out over my skin as he spoke. "You know what I meant," he purred against my chest moving his head from side to side, caressing my flesh with his lips. "What were you humming?"

Goosebumps broke out across my body as I moved my hands down his neck and across his broad shoulders.

My breath came in quick gasps as the heat inside me threatened to consume me. Pleasure coalesced within me and spread outward until every nerve ending throbbed for attention from him. "*Monsters* by Ruelle," I answered in a whisper as I twined my legs around his torso and curved into him like a flower opening to the sun. "You were having a nightmare. I thought it best to calm you rather than wake you."

"Hmmm. You think we are monsters?" He moved to my other nipple before peppering kisses up along my neck.

His breath was hot on my skin, and the delicious musk of our joint efforts permeated the space. I felt the head of his cock rub over my wet nether region, and I shivered in pleasure.

His lips were soft and inviting as he pressed them against mine, his tongue probing and exploring. I moved with him. Our rhythm matched as if we were two halves of a single creature.

"If that's what it takes to chase away your nightmares. Let me be your monster, Orion. Tell me what kind of devil you need. Tell me what you want right now."

I sensed turmoil in his thoughts by his pause and my mind threatened to fall into memories of the demon in my past.

"Be here with me. Right now." His words drew me back as his heavy body pressed me into the thin bed sheet beneath us. He raised himself up, removing the only source of friction from me.

"Be a bad girl," he growled, "and touch yourself."

My breath came in quick gasps when he commanded me to touch myself. What? I mean, what was the point if I had to do the work? "I prefer you do the touching."

"See, here's the thing. It would be an excellent form of evil torture if you denied me touching you. Made me watch you get off without me."

With a playful quirk of my lips, I said, "Really? Is it denying if you make the demand? Besides, I know you are watching. I will be performing for you. And I bet it would make you excited watching."

He growled and scowled at me, but it was a pitiful bit of pretend. "Are you my therapist or my love monster?"

I giggled very unmonster-like.

"Shit. Now I want to tickle you."

And he tickled me until my bladder was ready to burst. The rush of endorphins was a blessing and a different type of release I needed.

"Dani, you are gorgeous. Your smile outshines the sun and warms my cold shriveled heart."

"Your heart isn't shriveled and cold."

"Parts of it are."

I propped myself on my elbows and rubbed noses with him. "That's only because you're a grumpy pants."

He grunted and nosed me back. "Because you won't be mean to me." His lips brushed against my own and I got caught up in the beauty of his eyes. Dark blue veined with lighter, almost brownish blue and flecked with gray. A maelstrom to lure me in with a promise of destruction.

Orion wouldn't destroy me like Darius had tried. As bearish and grumpy as he sometimes could be, he was a softy.

My mouth turned up in a sly grin and I grazed my teeth delicately upon my lower lip, hoping I looked the epitome of sexy playfulness, my alluring actions, hinting at secrets yet to be revealed. More likely I just looked like a girl chewing on her lip.

Orion's eyes were glued to my mouth. Okay, so maybe I achieved alluring.

"I need you, Orion," I said, my voice husky and edged with desire.

He nipped at my neck and then kissed me hard, demanding. A teeth-knocking, tongue-sucking kiss. I wrapped my arms and legs around him.

Taking long licks down my neck, nipping and sucking away the pain, he growled. "Hands on yourself."

Caged by his arms, I grumbled but complied. My nerves fired electricity beneath my skin. His praise gave me the confidence to do as he asked.

With a deliberate, leisurely pace that masked my nerves as I played with myself. I skimmed my palms over the curve in my torso, circling my breasts.

His eyes flickered between my movements and my body. I splayed my legs and rolled my pelvis in a slow, sensuous motion. An invitation.

I released a quiet sigh. "Are you imagining being inside me?"

He hummed in appreciation. "How wet are you?"

Continuing my slow pace, I roamed my hands down my belly and over my thighs, skirting around my throbbing seam.

"You are so fucking sexy, baby. Perfectly perfect."

Finally, I grazed myself with my thumb. I was sopping. "You need me, don't you?"

"As much as air."

"How about a taste?" I swiped my thumb over his lower lip and he caught it with his teeth and sucked it into his mouth. The suction zinged all the way to my aching core.

He leaned in to kiss me again, and I moved my hips in response. My fingers found his long, hard, thick cock, and it quivered in my grip as I worked him through my folds.

"No, you don't," he said, his voice low and demanding. "Take care of that needy cunt."

I opened my eyes in shock, reliving a moment from my past. Darius used to call me a cunt frequently during sex. It was degrading for me to be reduced to nothing more than a honey hole to stick his dick into. Our sex life hadn't been about my pleasure, it was about his.

"Do you not care for that word, Dani?"

My eyes flickered to his. Orion. Not Darius. And Orion hadn't called *me* a cunt.

He leaned down next to my ear and sucked on my lobe. "Would you prefer I call it a needy pussy? You do mew like a kitten on occasion."

A flush of heat lit me up from the inside. "Pussy is good."

"Your pussy is not good, baby. It's fan-fucking-tastic, Dani. Please don't keep me waiting."

My body quivered while Orion continued speaking low to me, praising me with adoring words. I was Wild. Powerful. Beautiful. Untamed. Everything.

Listening to him was enough to take me to the edge. I needed more than his words, though. Something deep inside me needed the combination of his words with the comfort of his touch. I arched, my nipples scraped his chest, his sparse chest hair prickled my skin. That little bit fueled the fire within, and I finally slid my fingers through my slick center.

"That's my girl," he said.

I whimpered and hiked my legs higher, hooking one around his waist, my heel pressing into his ass. I slipped my other leg up and rested my knee against his biceps. Abandoning all sense of modesty, I gave in and worked my clit faster and faster, the naughty slippery noises in harmony with his ragged breathing.

My heart thundered in my chest as I felt my orgasm coiling tighter and tighter. My toes curled and my left foot began to cramp when Orion said, "Let go."

Let go. So simple really. Let go of everything holding me back. My fears and worries and to-do lists. Chores and job and wants. I let them all go.

"Dani. Look at me."

I opened my eyes and saw him staring at me with a fervid intensity, sparkling like two stars in an endless night sky.

"That's right. Fucking get off for me."

The pressure of my knee on his arm became my grounding point as every muscle in me contracted.

"Ahh," I cried out, unable to keep my eyes open.

His heat preceded the descent of his body into mine. Spasms continued to wrack through me as I felt him smack my clit with his dick.

"Again."

The smooth, abrupt slap was like a reset, a delicious, perfect hit to start me back up. He didn't do anything further, though. Restless for the friction of him inside me, I looked up at him. His face was strained in concentration, his eyes shut tight, skin gleaming with perspiration. I glanced between the gap of our bodies and saw him pinch himself just behind his glistening head. He mouthed a count of five.

I waited, then when he finally met my gaze, I whispered, my voice both low and assertive, "What are you waiting for, Orion? Fuck me. Hard."

His delightfully wicked grin said, *With absolute pleasure.* Damn, the exquisite sensations of him moving against me and into me were unlike anything I had ever experienced in my life. His soft grunt of pleasure along with his shallow breathing was a serenade I wanted to listen to on repeat.

But after a prolonged, blessed pause, he listened to my command and began driving into me with punishing energy, so hard the bed slammed into the wall as he thrust over and over.

Time and space meant nothing. The sounds of our skin slapping together, my soft gasps, the scent of him, his guttural grunts that were building in volume. He was everything, the cause of my body and soul being ripped apart as I came undone again.

"Oh God. O-Rion. Oh fuck!"

His incoherent shout rang out with one final pump. He twitched and jerked as he came inside me.

I ran my hand up his arms, his muscles bulging with tension. He lowered himself on me and I held him there. We shared the same space, the same air, our sweat mixed and mingled. His weight felt perfect, his heart thrumming in sync with my fluttering runaway organ.

"Please. Stay."

Lightheaded, extreme emotion overwhelmed me, and hot tears burned tracks over my temples. Orion kissed my shoulder, then pressed his cheek to mine.

I knew the chemicals, the hormones that raged for the moments to transpire, and yet the science behind the sex didn't take away from our bond.

THIRTY-TWO

ORION

Post-nut clarity is sometimes a cruel mistress. I didn't wish to withdraw, so instead of pulling out, I stayed just as I was.

Falling in love for me in the past happened without notice, a gradual or sudden awareness that this person was *it*. The one. When she said she'd be my monster and chase away the tortuous memories and fantasms, I fell so fucking hard it knocked me breathless.

No, this place was a blip. A pin on a map. This couldn't, wouldn't last. I didn't deserve her or her love or affection. In fact, she didn't deserve whatever it was I was doing to her.

Although I had found comfort here, in her arms, I knew it was only temporary.

This was not a place I deserved to stay in. I had nothing that could be of benefit to her, and the thought of that made me feel sick.

I couldn't tell her everything—my darkest secrets and scars—and let her see me stripped bare. A true demon.

I kissed gently along her neck in soothing circles before nibbling at her earlobe and whispering how beautiful she looked in my arms, and how perfect it felt being here with her like this. Her breathing changed from sob-like inhales to something longer and softer; with each exhale she relaxed more into me, a partnered dance of coming down from our high until eventually, our bodies settled into one another.

There was a depth to the emotion that stirred within me. Her gaze sent fire through every part of me, and I feared letting her go, so we stayed like that until our hearts and lungs no longer were frantic. Her inferno would consume me if I wanted to go along for the ride.

She shifted beneath me slightly, pushing her hips against mine, and before I even realized what she was doing, we were both suddenly shifting our weight in coordination with one another as we moved together in our intimately joined rhythm.

My erection was receding, but my girl was so hungry for more. Insatiable.

"Dani." I softly kissed her nose. "Baby, let me rest, please."

"Ah, my poor Marine needs a break." She kissed my forehead.

I had never focused so hard on one word before. *My.*

Mine.

I had never heard a sweeter word.

"Dani? What time is it?" Still beneath the covers, I had absolutely no idea.

"Coffee time. Let the puppy out time. Feed the birdies time. Feed Bunnie time."

"Feed the boyfriend time?" There. I said it. Offered my heart on a platter and waited to see if she would use a spoon to scoop it out onto the floor.

"I figured if I was doing all those chores, the boyfriend could feed me."

Her shy smile did things to me. Hard things. Woke the moths. Erased all the points and kicked us to a new level.

"Anything for you."

She raised a delicate eyebrow. "Anything?" Her voice came out breathy. "Hmm. I love the sound of that."

It turned out that besides the coffee, which I got on immediately, Dani did all the things she had mentioned, plus laundry, cleaned her bedroom, and started helping with breakfast.

"Eh, eh, eh? Shoo." I snapped her sweet ass with a damp kitchen towel. "I'm cooking."

"But—"

"Your butt is fine. And it should plant itself on the stool." I pointed to the island.

She managed an adorable pout but listened. I enjoyed her eyes on me as I moved through the kitchen.

When I was a kid, I helped my grandma in the kitchen as often as I could. It got me out of cleaning the bathroom and vacuuming. She taught me how to make bread, German dumplings, everything homemade.

I threw together my favorite breakfast. French toast crusted with a cinnamon/brown sugar glaze, stuffed with a peanut butter/cream cheese blend, and topped with fresh strawberries and hand-whipped cream. She didn't have "real" maple syrup, but we made do.

"This is fantastic, Orion. Oh, my gosh."

It had been a long time since I cooked for someone. I had forgotten how gratifying it could be.

Thor tried to convince me to share, but I resisted.

At one point while I cleaned up the dishes, Dani snuggled up behind me, nuzzling her face between my shoulders. Her arms around my waist felt like I owned a piece of heaven.

My phone vibrated in my back pocket.

"Oh. You got a live one in your pocket," she teased and rose on her tiptoes to nibble at my earlobe.

The woman drove all my worries into the shadows with her *everything*.

"Grab it for me, please. I should check to see who I'm ignoring."

"I sure hope you don't ignore my calls," she stage-whispered.

I raised my arm as I turned. Dani ducked beneath it, remaining wrapped about me. Her fingers clenched my phone as she gaped at the illuminated screen. "Holy crap, Rion. You have seventeen missed messages." She caught my gaze, her eyes blazing with disbelief. "Five from Courtney." Her voice had taken on a wary timbre. Knuckles whitening, she passed me my phone. She swallowed and stepped back. "You should probably read them. Might be an emergency."

I wanted to say something, but the reality of the situation had silenced my voice. Courtney was the last person I wanted to talk about, and yet, here we were.

Dani stood as if she already knew the answer. Before I could blink, she had already walked out of the room. Thor followed close behind. I wished I had the courage to do the same, but I stayed there, frozen.

Shit. I wasn't ready to go home, and I wasn't comfortable to say why. And Courtney? Ugh, no. She wasn't a great topic.

I found Dani in the shower of her bedroom with its oversized double-headed rain showerhead. She stood under the cascading water and I could see her tense as I entered.

She turned away from me, attempting to hide the pain that had replaced the smile from moments before. I felt my gut sink as I realized why—she knew Courtney wasn't a familial name.

The air in the room suddenly thickened, heavy with guilt, as I understood she had been waiting for me to explain; instead, I had remained silent, making myself an asshole.

"She's not who you think she is."

She looked over her shoulder, her eyes wide and her brows raised in surprise. "Oh? And exactly how could you know what I'm thinking?" Dani faced the wall again.

"No, I mean, she's... we're not close anymore." Orion felt the constriction in his throat, and he swallowed hard.

I watched her back tense, her fists balling at her sides, the steam from the shower rolling around her like a shroud. "That's alright, Orion. I don't need an explanation. You should do the right thing and contact your family—I sense they are really worried about you."

"See, I... I haven't told them about my discharge." I could practically hear the accusation in my own words, feel their weight as I heard her draw a deep breath and turn to face me, her dark eyes boring through the foggy barrier of the shower door.

"How long has it been? Since your discharge?"

I rubbed one hand over my hair, thinking. "About three months since I left Pendleton. Five since I received word of my superior's intent."

"Jesus, Orion. Why didn't you tell them? Surely if they knew, they would have..." Her words faded as she looked at me. Some part of my brokenness must have been showing.

"Maybe," I said. "I'm just not the same person anymore. I can't expect them to accept that part of me. Hell, I'm not even sure if I can."

Dani nodded slowly, a sad smile on her face. "Sometimes it takes a little courage to confront our ghosts, Orion. But if you don't, they'll stay with you, and they won't let go until you give them the closure they deserve."

I inhaled deeply, the steam of the shower swirling around me like a second skin. Dani remained standing in front of me, her face unreadable behind the shower door as she waited for me to say something more. I had to make things right between us. I knew that much.

"Dani," I began, my voice low and heavy with emotion. "I'm so sorry for not telling you about this." I gestured vaguely around us, to show my time in the military. "It wasn't right of me to keep it from you."

She nodded slowly, her face softening ever so slightly. "It's okay, Orion," she said, her voice gentle. "Really. We've only just met, but I feel this incredible connection." She released a wry laugh. "I know. Too soon. Look. I worry about you and want the best for you. Please believe me. I'll help you however I can."

My throat tightened as gratitude flooded through me and tears pricked at my eyes. She was giving me a chance—something that I didn't deserve—and it meant more than she could know.

"Thank you," I croaked out, my voice barely above a whisper as I met her gaze with mine own. For one long moment we simply stared at each other, there in the warm fog of water droplets—each searching for something in the other's eyes—until finally she gave a small nod and stepped outside, exiting the shower stall.

I stepped up and offered her a towel from the hook on the wall before following her into the bedroom, where she settled on the edge of the bed. She waved, indicating for me to do the same on a nearby chair. Sitting down across from her, I drew in another deep breath before bracing myself to tell her everything—to give someone else access to everything I had bottled up inside of me since leaving Pendleton months ago.

And so, with shaking hands and faltering words, I began pouring out some of my secrets, sharing more about my past with anyone I've ever known, except my counselor.

THIRTY-THREE

ORION

I sighed heavily. "After the last tour, I was in a really awful place. I didn't know how to get out of it, and I wasn't even sure I wanted to." I fingered my wrist unconsciously. "Your tattoo. Is it good to have it there as a reminder of what nearly happened?"

She sniffed. "Elliot or Eamon?"

I stayed silent, not feeling the need to rat out which brother felt the need to share such an intimate part of her past.

After a deep inhale, her gaze settled on her tattoo of a semicolon. "It's a reminder that it's okay to take a break. Reassess. It's not game over; it's just a pause. An interruption. And afterward, I found the strength to take the necessary steps to get back on track with life." Her smile had a distant quality as she spoke.

The woman sitting across from me had gone through her own horrors. Were we the same? Absolutely not. Should we try to fix each other? No.

A healthy dose of empathy, patience, and honesty would go a long way to help us as we healed. Honesty. I hung up on that word.

If I were to be completely honest with myself, I wanted to share everything with her. Tell her everything. Besides my counselors and doctors, she would learn what made me dysfunctional. Better to do it right away than scare her off after my heart was so deep in love that recovery from her running would be devastating.

She stared at me. Blinked. The silence stretched taut between us. I felt the energy build and build until my leg started bouncing.

"Say something. Please." I begged.

"Something. Please."

Irritation flashed through me as I realized her inability to take my confession seriously. Then I forced myself to calm down, reminding myself that becoming an ass was not the best thing to do. Dani handled things differently than I did.

"Orion? Look at me, please."

Our eyes met, and I could feel an energy between us. She asked me something I didn't expect. "Do you want me to sit with you while you call them?"

I struggled between accepting her offer and not wanting anyone to witness my vulnerability. But Dani wasn't anyone. I blinked away my confusion and nodded.

"Give me a second. Why don't you get dressed, too? In case you want to video chat."

I pulled on a tee, and my skivvies, then sat on the couch, waiting for Dani. She followed, wearing a white tank top and baby blue shorts, her hair pulled back into a low ponytail. "Okay." She clasped her hands together and vigorously rubbed them. "Ready?"

"No."

She smiled and kissed me. The peck turned into a deeper exploration. "I believe in you," she said.

Thank God because I lacked faith in myself.

I stared at the phone in my hand, willing the courage to make the call. The thought of all the people unknowingly waiting for me to take a risk weighed on me as did all the times I had told myself that it was impossible.

Then I considered all the risks I had already taken in life. I could not allow my fear to stop me from moving on.

I dialed my parents' number and turned on the camera, deciding I needed to face them for this conversation.

My heart felt like a clump of lead in my chest. I wanted so desperately for them to answer and to not answer, both at the same time. I had so much to say, but I wasn't sure where to start. With every passing second, my confidence diminished more and more. I stared down at my hands, trying to find strength from deep within.

I watched Dani's hand slip into mine. Her warmth grounded me. Finally, someone picked up.

"Hello?" came a voice from the other end of the line.

I took a deep breath and spoke. "Mom?"

"Orion! Wait a minute, please. Let me get this thing here... okay? Orion? Can you see me? Hear me?"

My mom's smiling face appeared, and it was all I could do not to break down and bawl. Her dark hair had more silver streaks in it from the last time I saw her. Her brown, warm eyes gazed at me from the screen, her glasses pushed up on her head, holding her straight, long hair back from her face. Dani gave my hand a squeeze.

As I opened up to my mother and shared an abbreviated version of what had occurred in the past months, Dani reached down and picked Thor up, placing him in her lap. She played with him while I spoke.

"Oh, honey. I love you so much. I've been worried about you. With how long it has been since we last spoke, I knew something was up."

"I am sorry I waited so long to call."

"That's all right. Your dad and brother made a few calls several months ago. Got in touch with a couple of your buddies. They told us a bit. I knew you would find me when you were ready."

My tears welled up, and I brushed my eyes. Dani was right there with a tissue.

Thor crawled over to me and licked my chin before he sniffed my phone.

"A puppy? Is he yours? What's his name?" Mom asked as she pulled her glasses from her head and wiped her own eyes. Her bangs fell over her forehead in a soft wave.

"Mom. I would like you to meet Thor. I found him a few weeks ago, as lost, beat up, and lonely as me."

"Oh, sweetheart. Thor is adorable."

Thor agreed and tried to tongue-punch my mom, only to get the screen.

I mouthed to Dani, "Do you want to meet my mom?"

A smile slowly spread across her face. She winked and nodded.

"Mom? I have someone else to introduce you to."

"That lion behind you?" Mom pointed, and I turned.

Bunnie perched majestic-like behind me. I had no idea the cat had snuck up on us. What a sneaky bugger.

I laughed. "Yes. That is Bunnie. And no. I don't think he will eat me. Mom, this is Dani."

Dani leaned in and waved. "Hello, Mrs. Windwalker. Nice to meet you."

Mom's eyebrows attempted to disappear into her silver bangs. "Dani. Nice to meet you."

"I'm Thor's vet and Orion's..." She turned to me. "What am I?"

"You are everything, Dani."

THIRTY-FOUR

ORION

After talking more with Mom, she told me Dad wasn't home. "He's out in the boat, trying to get one more day in before he has to put it away and break out the icehouse."

The thought of battered and fried walleye made my mouth water and my stomach rumble.

"We would be happy to get you a ticket home so you can visit, Orion. I would love to baby my boy for as long as you can spare me."

The idea sounded great. Better to talk to Dad first, so I knew the lay of the land.

"Dani and Thor are welcome as well."

"Thanks, Mom. I'll think about it. Tell Dad to call me when he gets a chance."

"Dani? It was nice to meet you. Please make sure my son turns his phone ringer on."

Dani's laugh was like a refreshing mist behind a rainbow. "I'll try but can't promise anything."

After I hung up, I leaned back onto the couch, feeling lighter than I had in months.

"See? You did it."

"Yeah." I ran a hand over the top of my head. "My mom is easier than my dad."

Dani picked Thor up off my lap and set him beside me. She then crawled into his place; knees parked on either side of my thighs. I lost myself in her kiss.

"Orion. Are you ready to tell me who Courtney is?" Dani rested her forehead against mine.

So, there I was, feeling better for talking to my mom, and had a beautiful woman with whom my soul was melting into a puddle in her hands. One more truth to reveal.

"Courtney is a girl from my past. Someone I would rather forget about," I finally admitted. The memories filled me with a mix of emotions, feelings I hadn't allowed myself to feel for so long. It had been so easy to bury them down deep inside myself, but now here they were on the surface, raw and painful. "During those first few nights after I learned I would receive a medical discharge, instead of calling my family, I called her. A moment of stupidity during a night I tried to erase my nightmares in liquor." She took my call as a sign of more things to come.

I could tell that Dani was disappointed by the change on her face. I could see it in her eyes and I felt her body tense up against me. Instinctively, I held her, but she hid her emotions beneath the mask of a stone-cold face. I wanted to say something to make it better, but nothing came out of my mouth.

Then she exhaled. "I don't judge you for who or what you did before me. We both have our pasts. But Rion, please deal with her so we can move on without—" she waves a hand between us. "One more piece of baggage."

The air between us hung heavy and oppressive as if each word could burst into flame and ignite an argument. Each passing second dug us deeper into an abyss of distance. My heart raced and my palms grew clammy. I wanted to bridge the gap between us by explaining why Courtney was messaging me, but I couldn't muster enough courage, and I honestly had no idea why she continued to pester me. I hadn't felt remorse before over ignoring Court, but now I faced a reckoning.

"Does she know she's your ex?" Dani's question was so soft I almost didn't hear it.

My forehead creased. "Yes."

"I'm only asking because of all the notifications from her."

Ah yes, the notifications. "She was never one to leave things alone."

Dani held up a hand in protest. "Sorry. I'm being a jealous girlfriend when I know this is only a distraction. It's none of my business."

"But—" The panic that had been brewing rose to choke me as I desperately wanted her to understand. "Dani. I wasn't lying when I said you are everything." My voice broke on the last word.

She smiled, but it was a sad smile that didn't quite reach her eyes. "But we don't even know each other. We've only breached the surface." Dani murmured.

I wanted to agree because she was correct. But would she deny feeling an incredible connection to me as I did to her?

"Do you want to?" I waited, my heart pounding even though the moths in my gut hid away, afraid.

We lapsed in silence, my thoughts tumbling over and over like a never-ending cycle. I hoped she said yes because turning back time to undo the past few days was an impossibility.

Dani's gaze met mine. The room filled with silent tension as I waited for her to say something, anything. Her expression wavered between uncertainty, understanding, and respect, all as if she was seeing me for the first time.

"Yes," she finally said in a whisper.

THIRTY-FIVE

DANI

He introduced me to his mom. An absurd giddiness bubbled in my chest leaving me breathless and I wanted to bask in the development. Not just to be introduced, obviously, but for him to take such a tremendous step.

Keeping his discharge a secret from his family gnawed on his conscience like a greedy puppy.

Scratch that.

Thor chewed on my hands and feet, clothes and hair to bond, ease teeth pain, and be tactile.

No, Orion's secret would be better described as a heavy boa constrictor wrapping his entire body, head to toe, and tightening in slow and constant increments.

He showed the weight of relief he felt in the easing of tension in his shoulders and the more natural curl of his mouth. He didn't talk more or spill stories about his life.

He mellowed. Bummed around. Tinkered.

It was... relaxing.

And simultaneously sexy as hell.

The thought that "a twice bright flame burns half as long" could be exactly what was occurring between us. A douse of pessimism punched me in the gut. I agreed to what? Testing the waters more thoroughly? The fact he wandered into my path was still fact. He had no place to go, no future plan. I wasn't sure if our relationship should give him direction. He needed to sort his life out on his own. My neck prickled over a name... Courtney. Who was she and why wouldn't Orion talk about her? An ex. Someone from his past.

Did that mean Courtney meant more or less than the other things?

I reminded myself that it didn't matter. He was here with me. Whatever he had done before made him into the man at my side, who, I reminded myself, I still knew very little about.

Knowing my own insecurities and the cold bitter road I'd stumble down if I allowed myself to think too long or hard about it, I selected a distraction. I asked Orion if he could show me his uniform.

We stood facing each other in the loft in the cottage. I read a scene in a book about a couple enjoying each other surrounded by mirrors. A memorable scene, to be sure. My cottage had several large mirrors to help with light reflection in the dark A-frame, two of which I planned to use. He caught on when I asked him to help me carry a full-length one up from downstairs. Propped against the chest of drawers and angled just so with the other tall mirror, he could see us from the side or, as I planned, watch my back as I knelt before him.

I didn't know anything about this Courtney person, but since Orion was with me, I wanted to make him think only of me. Of us.

At the moment, he stood dressed in his uniform. When I asked him to wear it for me, I read his hesitancy for what it was. Fear. Reluctance. Shame.

"You are still a Marine. And, you are not broken, merely bent and in need of a polish." I cocked an eyebrow and dragged my eyes pointedly down his body while licking my lips. I could feel the blush that warmed my cheeks, certain the fire in my belly could light up my entire body in a ghastly red.

He allowed me to assist by removing the few scraps of clothing, insisting I stand naked in front of one mirror so we could watch while his hands skimmed my curves. It took a lot of effort to stand there and not try to cover up or hide parts of myself.

"You are gorgeous." His breath caressed my ear, erupting a wash of goosebumps over my flesh and heating my core.

It's safe to say I've been in heat since I met him, and I wasn't sure when I would go out... probably when he left. What would remain? A cooling pile of once molten woman?

Best not to think such things when he eye-fucked every inch of my body.

"You are perfect for me."

The man knew what to say, and when to say it, I'd give him that. And the devastating look on his face made my soul swell and a savage moan escaped me.

My heart flipped and flopped beneath his hooded gaze. It's one thing to feel your partner touching you. But to watch it happen, witness his eyes devouring my figure as his rough palms brazenly moved across my planes, and see my body's response was an intensely intimate and erotic thing. I damn near orgasmed without him touching me between my legs.

His hands gripped my waist, tightening his hold and suddenly, frantically, I needed more than just his body.

I needed everything.

Throwing my arm up and behind his head like Baby did for Johnny in Dirty Dancing, I pulled his head to mine and dragged my mouth over his. His chest heaved with his ragged breathing and everything inside of me bloomed into motion. We matched each other move for move, tongue for tongue.

Squeezing my thighs together did nothing to stave off the ache that built, the ache that demanded friction.

Not yet. I had a plan and damned if I wasn't going to fulfill it.

"Put on your uniform, Orion."

"Yes, ma'am."

His soft words caused the heat pooling between my legs to release, like a dam exploding between swollen, needy riverbanks.

I leaned back against the closet door, my hands resting on the smooth wood, and watched him with hungry eyes as he changed. In his dress blues, I admired his rumpled hair, full lips, and now concealed erection. He looked every bit like a meal and dessert.

It was a known fact of life—men in uniform had a certain je ne sais quoi that made them magnetic, no matter the age. The crisp uniforms showcased strength, stability, and security—things many sought in life. Things I sought for myself. Wearing it, he embodied authority and power, and nothing was more attractive to me than a man who could take charge and care for his own. I pretended he was prepared to care for me. I should be realistic, but preferred fantasy.

His blue Marine uniform may have been simple, but what it represented when Orion wore it was far from simple. A navy blue coat with his rankings and medals, white belt, and blue pants with a red stripe.

A selfless hero.

I stepped close and traced an insignia on his sleeve, three chevrons and a bursting bomb.

Orion filled the blanks in my questioning mind. "That chevron is for the rank of Gunnery Sergeant. Or Gunney."

The next patch I touched was a skull wearing a green beret, a knife gripped in its teeth upon a black shield.

"My Marine Raiders division patch."

"Raiders," I murmured. I tapped the medal on the left side of his chest over his heart. "Purple heart."

He grunted and made a motion with his chin. "These are my service stripes. One for each year."

I fingered the colorful strips. His face remained passive, but I could practically taste his disappointment. My eyes skimmed over the other patches.

There was weight to the garment, though it wasn't from the material but from what he had faced as a Marine. What he carried on his shoulders. I imagined the smell of gunpowder, a subtle odor of warfare that was purely psychological as he never wore this garment in combat.

All the while I inspected his uniform, he stared determinedly into the distance, avoiding my gaze while I eye-fucked him.

My throat tightened knowing the unease that shadowed his heart over his perceived eviction from the inner circle of his brethren. I automatically respected and admired his service, even if it was too short by Orion's standards. His presence alone brought me a sense of peace and comfort.

All of a sudden, his palpable discomfort left a bitter taste in my mouth, and I second-guessed my request for him to wear it for me.

"What now, beautiful?" Orion quipped with a cocksure grin, bringing me out of my slip into dark thoughts.

Such a good Marine.

"Just watch." I made a shh gesture with my finger pressed to his lips. "Don't move. No touching."

With careful slowness, I unbuttoned his coat, avoiding actively touching him. After removing it from his broad shoulders, I took my time putting it back on the hanger and placing it in the closet.

I felt his gaze on me like a physical caress. When I exaggerated my postures for his benefit, did I also look in the mirrors or over my shoulder to see his response? Absolutely. I enthralled him.

Turning back to him, I tugged at his plain white tee, pulling it out from his waistband.

"Enjoying the show this far?" I asked, my voice husky from desire. I had a very sensitive itch that required scratching with his engorged cock.

Not. Yet.

Orion moistened his lips, then said, "Yes."

I raised my eyebrows.

His eyes darted to the mirror behind me, and I wiggled my ass for him. "You are—"

"Going to suck you off. Now, be a good Marine, and let me worship you."

Kneeling at his feet, I took my time undoing his belt. Then his zipper. My attention moved between what I was doing and his face. His intense look had my heart and soul doing flip-flops. My mouth watered in anticipation of drawing him into it and lavishing attention solely on him. For him.

His length sprung free of its confines, and I ran my tongue along the underside ribbed with engorged veins. I gazed up through my lashes to see he looked at me with reverence and adoration. Many, many times over the last few days, he looked at me with a contorted, jacked-up expression of it-feels-so-good-but-is-g-d-painful face, but his expression now topped the charts.

Did he feel as strongly for me, or was this a way to pass the time for him? Had we trauma bonded or was the look on his face a true reflection of devotion? Infatuation or the opening blossoms of love?

More importantly, did it matter?

I realized it mattered very much.

THIRTY-SIX

ORION

Never in the history of "Orion's Sexual Escapades" had something like this ever happened to me.

A blow job while in uniform.

I've heard my brothers brag about it, but this was not an act I would ever boast about. Treasure—absolutely. Replay it often. Dani on her knees and lavishing attention on me made me feel honored and invincible.

Yeah, I get it. Hot chick on her knees, blah blah.

I hadn't asked nor was it the first time her lips graced my rod.

But the mirrors and her naked body and my uniform... Hot. Very hot.

This woman, though, was the one for me. When I pictured my future plans, Dani fit like a puzzle piece at my side.

Pulling me back to the moment, she gripped my base with both hands, pumping and wringing as she sucked and tongued absolute bliss from me. Her carnal sensuality wafted about in the air currents and as soon as she swallowed me dry, I needed to taste her and hear my name on her lips.

The mirrors were fantastic, and we used them well. Not only did I watch her from every angle possible, I asked her to do the same.

I knew for a fact that we were both weary and desensitized after all the incredible, mind-blowing sex, but every time still felt new. Incredible.

Maybe a little soreness factored in, but she took everything I gave her for another hour until we collapsed together. Again.

THIRTY-SEVEN

ORION

Monday came too quickly. Dani dropped me off at Elliot's shop on her way to work, which was out of the way, but she insisted. We planned to meet for lunch if she had time. I waited patiently in front of the shop for Elliot. Connie the Conure parrot honked at me from her perch. She had no intention of getting close to me and resisted my attempts to have her step onto my finger.

He had opened it early for us and came out with a big grin. "Come on back. I want to show you something."

Thinking he had a muscle car or motorcycle to show off, I followed. Thor bumbled alongside, sniffing the very tidy garage.

A sharply detailed '72 Ford Bronco sat in the center of the shop.

"Where the hell did you find one for yourself?" I whistled, taking in the beautiful paint job. Thor pawed my leg in agreement.

Then I noticed the license plate.

"Before you get pissed or say something stupid, it was Dani's idea. And you don't owe me anything."

My god. The Bronco looked brand new. A well of emotion threatened to roll me.

Elliot approached and slapped me on the shoulder. "She really likes you, man. Do not fuck with her."

Feeling shaky, I offered him a smile.

Eamon walked in from the back. "So? What do you think?"

"It's incredible. Thank you. Both of you."

Eamon shrugged. "Thanks for staying with Dani. She took the most recent encroachment rather well."

The back of my neck prickled as anger edged out my mushier emotions. "Recent? When was the last time?"

Eamon squatted and held a hand out to Thor. Uncertain, Thor clung to my leg, although his tail wiggled. I gave him a gentle nudge, encouraging him. Thor, hunched almost like he needed to take a shit, sidestepped toward Eamon.

"Hey, big guy. I bet my sister loves on you more than Orion."

Laughing, I said, "I can openly admit to never being jealous of a dog before Thor." I lifted my eyebrows and crossed my arms. "You know how she is."

They updated me on Dani's ex, basically informing me there were no new developments.

"The back camera on?"

I nodded.

Eamon stood, Thor in his arms. "So, now that I finished repairing your truck, what are your plans?"

"I don't really have any." I paused, going over my recent thoughts.

"No job somewhere? Home to return to?"

They looked at me expectantly. By their open faces, I assumed Dani hadn't shared my story.

"Nope. I recently got out of the Marines. Trying to figure out what to do next."

"New chapter, huh? Are you good with your hands?"

"Your sister thinks so." The words were out of my mouth before I realized it. Blood drained from my face as what I implied slammed into my gut, awakening a horde of moths with steel-tipped wings.

Eamon laughed, his entire body joining in the action. Elliot pursed his lips, trying not to smile. Shit, I was glad they had a sense of humor like their sister.

Clearing my throat, I said, "I'm pretty good with engines. Oil changes. Electrical shit."

"I have been short a guy for a couple of months. I'm willing to train what you don't know if you will work." Elliot, fierce Elliot, had the hopeful look of someone who discovered he may have won the lottery.

"At my age, I can only surf so much. A job would be excellent."

And so it went. For several weeks, my life settled into a new routine. Work. Dani. Life.

During her next bout of after-hours on-call, I rode along. Thor accepted his new kennel for the times he couldn't go with. Some nights were non-stop calls and visits, and others were quiet. I drove so she could rest and took naps over my lunch. It was perfect.

What they say about life is true. Life is an unpredictable roller-coaster with severe ups and downs and steep curves. Anticipation. Fear. It can steal your breath from gravity or other forces.

For the next several weeks, we lived on a high.

The up was bound to end sooner than later.

THIRTY-EIGHT

ORION

The second round of Dani's two-week emergency rotation I lived through with her was even more exhausting than the first. It didn't help that she received strange hang-ups and mysterious messages from unknown numbers that left us both uneasy. The PI keeping tabs on her ex hadn't any news, although I suspected it was Darius, or Dickface. Her brothers' nickname for the guy clung better to the image I had created in my mind.

Her temper frayed, and before long, a week passed with no intimacy. But I refused to attempt anything, preferring instead to just hold her close as she slept.

Worry consumed my thoughts; nightmares of head-on collisions, of falling off cliffs kept me up late and exhausted my sleep. I feared for her safety every time she stepped out into the night.

I guess I should have been relieved I wasn't reliving my last tour every night. This was almost worse.

No. It was worse.

She was in survival mode. We both were.

"This isn't good, Dani. Can't your boss hire relief?" I had been researching the veterinary profession. Because of an overwhelming number of factors, the job had one of the highest suicide rates, over four times higher than the general population. Sleep deprivation alone can lead to suicidal thoughts in those without a history of mental illness. Although I had a glimpse into the life of a veterinarian, I couldn't imagine carrying the weight of emotional attachment to each animal, and the depth of responsibility Dani held regarding her patients, clients, and team. Dani wasn't struggling financially, but vets often carried a heavy student loan debt and didn't make a comparative salary to offset that expense.

"I don't know if there are any available."

No one should have to suffer through this as often as she did. "Could you suggest it?"

She exhaled a groan. "I have. There isn't anyone."

"This is not healthy."

"You're right." She booped my nose with hers. "But it is temporary." At my raised eyebrows, she continued, "You don't have to go with me."

"I want to, though."

"Why bother, if it's interrupting your life?"

"You are my life, Dani." I realized how true those words were and it terrified me. The Marines had been my life, and I became lost without them. What would I do if I lost her?

She was saying, "Orion?" over and over. When she caught my attention, she continued, "I can't let them down."

At what point did her goal in life change from working a job she enjoyed to one where she was more concerned about her team than her health?

It was like she was in the military.

"You're a doctor, for Christ's sake. Human doctors don't have these hours."

"That's probably true. But this is my job."

"And it's not worth your sanity or your life, Dani."

Something I said triggered her. I saw it in the way her body stiffened, her nostrils flared.

"I'm sorry. The last thing I want to do is tell you what to do." I tugged her rigid body close to me. "I'm worried as fuck about you."

She let me hold her until she relaxed, then fell asleep. I lay there in the darkness, listening to the ticking of the clock.

Losing her would not be something I could come back from. Fuck. I hadn't known her for long, but she was a part of my life. A part of me.

I needed her to know that.

We hadn't used the L word. Why did that bother me?

Once she woke and thanked me for not pushing her for sex when she was tired. *Thanked me.*

"You expect me to push you for sex?"

"Isn't that a man's love language?"

"I am no man, baby, I'm the Greek Hunter. I'm prepared to wait until the time is right. You can say no. I'm not able to read your mind, you know."

"I can say no? You won't pout or degrade me for not putting you first?"

Wait. What? "Why would..." Her eyes glistened, and she glanced away. Fuck. That son-of-a-bitch. "Dani. Look at me."

When her eyes met mine, it was like looking into a mirror. Uncertainty, vulnerability, and hope stared back.

"I love you."

Her eyes widened in surprise before transforming into an elated smile. "I love you too," she replied, her lips brushing lightly against mine.

I held her close, savoring the moment of pure bliss, before resting my head on top of hers. I never wanted to be apart from her... ever. In the brief time since she ran into me, Dani became my world, and I loved every second with her by my side.

The sun continued to set, and our days passed quickly. Every moment shared was something I cherished more than anything else I had ever known before. Sorry, not sorry for the extra serving of cheese.

The morning of the last night of her emergency rotation came, and I took the following day off to take care of her.

On one hand, I worried about smothering her. On the other hand, I didn't want to miss a moment.

Our lovemaking that morning surpassed expectations. With each time being better than the last, I wondered at what point my world would implode.

I said, "You're mine, baby."

"Yours."

"And I'm yours."

"Mine," she whimpered. "Fuck, Orion. You're mine."

I maintained a slow pace, pausing when I felt myself get too close. Our hands clasped above her head.

"We fit perfectly."

"So good." She panted, rolling her hips faster, using the friction from my pelvis to edge her closer.

"You're incredible. Beautiful." I continued whispering encouragement and praise. "That's my girl."

As her orgasm ripped through her, she let out a guttural, stuttered moan of pleasure. The arch of her body against mine and the tight contractions of her pussy were almost too much to bear. I thrust hard and fast, pistoning my hips. She begged for more and I obliged, pushing us both closer to the brink of bliss.

My vision tunneled and all I could see was her face—lips parted, eyes closed in ecstasy, damp locks of hair sticking to her forehead—as I felt my abdomen clench and I slammed into her one last time, grunting with each powerful pulse of my dick.

"Damn, Dani," I murmured against her skin. "I love you."

THIRTY-NINE

ORION

An awful buzzing roused me from sleep. Dani spooned in my arms. I didn't want to move, but the buzzing continued ceaselessly. And I had to piss.

I grabbed my phone off the nightstand and worked my unsteady way to the head. 3:47 p.m. We had slept away most of the day. I was glad we had fed everyone when we got home. Thor was probably crossing his legs. Or worse, wasn't. I didn't really want to clean up a mess.

The caller's name popped up on my phone.

Courtney.

I declined the call and sent a message I would call her back.

I wouldn't.

After taking Thor out, we both wandered back into the bedroom. Dani, awake, watched me walk in.

"Hey, handsome." She gave me a soft smile. "Come here."

I climbed in and pulled her on top of me.

"I let Thor out." I tucked her hair behind her ears as she crossed her hand over my chest and rested her chin upon them.

She raised a dainty eyebrow. "Naked?"

"Yes."

"But I turned the back cameras on." She bit back a laugh.

I stretched my arms out overhead. "No worries. I took him out the front."

She blew a raspberry on my chest, knowing full well I didn't go out the front, nor had she turned the back cameras on.

I rolled, pinning her beneath me, and found her weak spots. My fingers danced over her skin, and she squirmed and laughed until tears ran from her eyes. Her wriggling and writhing amped up my constant need for her but I focused on this different type of euphoria. Her smile stole my breath and made me yearn to do anything to see it over and over again.

Her carefree howls and cackles filled me with as much pleasure as her body moving beneath me.

Pausing, I kissed her forehead. "Time to eat. I'll make a late lunch, or early supper, I guess. It's almost four."

A yawn nearly split her face.

"Why don't you stay here and rest some more?" I suggested as I crawled off.

She pouted, her hands grabbing for me. Just then, her phone vibrated.

"Ugh. Throw that piece of shit away."

"Such language." I poked her in the ribs.

"What are you going to do? Spank me?"

The thought had crossed my mind before, but with her history, there was no way I ever would without her asking, scratch that, begging for it.

I winked. "Maybe I should."

She sat up and leaned into me. "Hmm, sounds like fun."

"So these books you read..." I smiled into her rat's nest of hair. "They aren't only to live vicariously through. They're what, prep? Research?"

I knew the kinds of books she read because I had read some of them. I learned a few things, too, and applied them in the bedroom. Or the kitchen. Living room. Wherever I had an opportunity. Dani thoroughly enjoyed everyone.

Other than fucking so hard we scratched the paint of the wall behind her headboard, I had attempted no BDSM. Perhaps we could have that conversation now.

Her phone vibrated again, and she flopped backward with a groan. My eyes caught on the jiggle of her plump breasts, and I suddenly wanted to burrow my face between them. So I did.

Her phone buzzed. Again.

"Check who it is, please. Then shut it off."

Gladly. I knew she was worried about work getting in touch with her. I also knew the world kept spinning.

"Hello?" I answered without checking.

There was a pause, then a male voice said, "Who's this?"

"It's Orion. Dani is unavailable. Can I take a message?"

A beat of silence followed, and my eyes flickered to Dani. The hair rose on the back of my neck.

"You tell that whore I'm coming for her."

Then the call ended, as did my elated buzz.

"We need to turn the back cameras on now." After I shared what the caller had said, we walked out into the kitchen. I pulled on my skivvies and a tee while she, wearing a tank and sweats, called her parents.

They asked her to stay with them for a while.

"I have my pets here, Mom. I can't leave them, and I certainly can't allow Sasha to come over if I'm not here."

Her anxiety bled over into the kitchen where we sat but failed to reach Thor, who chewed on a toy at my feet. Bunnie sat sentinel on the kitchen island. That cat taught me to Clorox kitchen surfaces before cooking.

"Okay. I'll talk with Rion and get back to you."

She rested her face in her hands, the muscles of her forearms flexing seemingly in time with my heartbeat. Her knee bounced below the table.

"We could go visit my parents' place," I suggested. "He wouldn't know to go there."

"And what if he did?" Her sad voice tore at my heart.

We would take care of it, I thought.

My phone rang, and I checked the screen. Declined the call.

"Who was that?" Dani asked without lifting her head.

I didn't answer immediately. Courtney had become a thorn.

Thor groaned and flopped on his side, slipping into a power nap. Bunnie dropped gracefully to the floor and approached, sniffing my pup, before laying down at Thor's back.

"Orion."

I jerked back into myself. "What?"

"You need to deal with Courtney."

"There's nothing to deal with."

She gave me a pointed look. "Obviously there is, if she is still calling." Her face fell. "Unless you don't want her to stop." Fear and confusion warred on her stricken face.

"No. I do. Want her to stop."

Her eyebrows dipped. "Then why don't you talk to her?"

Why indeed? I texted her instead. *Please stop trying to contact me. I'm not interested.*

"I'd rather not," I began, trying to find the words to reassure Dani.

My phone rang.

"Answer it, for fuck's sake." Anger edged Dani's tone.

She was right. I needed to face it.

"Courtney," I greeted her.

"Orion, I'm so sorry to bother you. I don't know what else to do."

I placed the phone on speaker, wanting Dani to hear what I said and Courtney's response, so the one I loved knew I tried.

"Courtney, I'm not interested in a relationship with you."

"I know, Rion. I know." Her voice wavered as she spoke. "But I'm pregnant. And it's yours."

My whole body froze when she uttered those words.

"No. It can't be."

"You're the only one I've been with, Rion."

The possibility outweighed the probability at that point. I didn't want to be a dad, not with her.

Dani, poor Dani. I sensed her disbelief and heartbreak. A pregnancy would change a lot of things. I didn't know what to say, and every part of me wanted to deny it.

Remember my injury? "No, it's not. I'm infertile. Besides, the last time I saw you, I wore protection."

"Orion, you were too drunk to realize what you were doing. You didn't use a condom!" She choked on a sob and I felt guilty.

But then I shook my head again in disbelief. "I'm infertile. I can't have kids. I shoot blanks." My words came slowly, almost as if to reassure myself.

"Then why wear a condom?"

"To prevent something like this. Who else have you been with? You need to call them instead."

"It's only been you!" she shrieked. "I'm not a slut!"

My heart pounded, and I could sense my blood pressure spike. I restrained myself from saying that was exactly what I thought of her, the very reason I'd called her a few times in the past. A few of my buddies had suggested her, not that they had experienced her, but that she liked to hang out where we did.

"Courtney, you need to rethink this. I can't be the father."

"Can't or don't want to be?"

My stomach twisted in knots, and I felt bile rise in my throat from the words that slithered from Courtney's lips. I sensed Dani's gaze as I fumbled for an explanation.

I stuttered a reply, a feeble attempt to throw out an explanation, when Dani mouthed, "Are you one hundred percent certain?" Her eyes drilled into me with a mix of concern, shock, and resignation.

I nodded solemnly before shrugging my shoulders in defeat.

"Fix this," she commanded, her finger pointing toward me before she spun around and marched out of the room.

Fuck. When it rains, it pours. What had Dani said when I first met her? Bad things happen in threes and sevens? This was number two, right? Darius—one. Courtney—two. What would be the third?

FORTY

DANI

I walked away, no longer able to listen to the frantic, panicked faceless woman on the phone begging Orion.

Pregnant.

His recount of his testicular injury surfaced, and I weighed the probabilities.

Although low, there was still a chance. Men with surgical vasectomies have impregnated women.

Life finds a way. I rolled my inner eyes at the reference to Ian Malcolm from *Jurassic Park*.

Where did this revelation leave my relationship with the man of my dreams? The man I could totally picture alongside me in my future?

A distraction.

A source of entertainment.

A pit stop on his trip through life.

Were these things all that I was to him?

Another Courtney?

I reminded myself, *No. You were the one to send him away, Dani.*

How sad those sardonic voices in my head questioned my feelings for him. I believed he cared for me. Truly. Or perhaps our flare was flickering out.

This other woman—Courtney—and Orion had a thing, and it took precedence over our relationship. *Theirs* happened before *ours.*

A swell of anger washed over me leaving a flush of heat. He needed to take care of his shit. My empathy and patience went so far, and I already felt strung so tight, my edges fraying. When would I break?

I needed time. He would be unsafe with me, anyway. Darius would... What would Darius do? He used to hurt me. Had accused me of sleeping with practically everyone I had worked with when we were together. But he never hurt anyone else. There had never been anyone else. Only me. Great way to alienate the insecure, needy girl I had been.

Terror over the possibility Orion could get hurt made me feel sick. What if Darius hurt Orion? Fuck. What if Orion got re-tangled with Courtney, honor-bound to care for a child? Where would that leave us?

My mind raced with possibilities, my heart beating faster with every thought. I needed to protect him from Darius first and foremost so he could have the opportunity to be a dad.

A shuddering wave of terror rushed over me, forcing me to confront the truth I had been too afraid to face. In that moment, I knew he might never be transparent enough with me to meet my needs. We were like two delicate spiders spinning a web of protection, a barrier to protect our jagged edges, one misstep away from total destitution and darkness. Sorrow invaded my entire body with an uncontrollable force, and only one thing could make it better—calling my dad.

"Hello, sunshine."

His warm, caring voice broke something inside me.

"Danica? Dani, are you safe?"

Are you safe, not *are you alright*? Daddy knew the right words to use.

"I'm safe," I said, my chest heaving with a poorly suppressed sob.

He sat with me, the soothing sounds of surf accenting the quiet. Either he was on the beach, or he played ocean sounds for me. He knew the calming effect they had on me. My father rarely pushed. He had the patience of a Saint.

When I could talk, I updated him on the turnings of my love life.

"You're right. Orion needs to address this development. If I was a betting man, I would wager Orion isn't the father. But a paternity test will settle that."

"I just wish he would have told me," I sniffed.

"Told you he slept with other women? Did you believe you had taken his virginity then?"

His bluntness brought out a sharp laugh from me. "No."

"And did you share intimate details of your sexual history?"

"Okay. Fine. I understand. Doesn't make me question less."

"Yes, but how worthy are the speculations of your time and energy, Danica? Your focus should be on your health. Your sleep. Food. Exercise. What's your work schedule for the week?"

And so, my dad talked me through my week. He told me about one of my nephew's exploits in a surfing competition. About Mom's hairstyle still catching him off guard. "My gut stabs with worry every time I see her with that short hair that your mom will find out a strange woman is in our house or caught my attention."

"You think Mom is hot. That's both endearing and unsettling."

"Why? Because people our age aren't supposed to be sexy or have sex?"

I gave a noncommittal grunt, happy to have my thoughts appeased. Everything had scrubbed a heavy hand against my fur, and my father easily smoothed it back into line.

"Tell Orion I will help however I can, but that he better not hurt you. Your brothers live only minutes away."

I smile despite the silly threat. My family attacked with the fury and solid hand of the law. It was Darius who seemed hellbent on intimidating and harassing me, mere steps away from physical harm, something my body recalled too clearly.

FORTY-ONE

ORION

Courtney's pregnancy fit the timeline of the last time I saw her. Still.

"I need you to do a paternity test. Immediately. Please. I'll drive down if I have to and take you."

Her anguished sigh spoke volumes, and I hazarded a guess she had heard the request already.

"Courtney. Please be honest. Am I the only potential father?"

A long silence filled the line until I could make out sniffling.

"Courtney? Are you there? Can you hear me?"

"Yes. I'm so sorry. No. You aren't. The only one. I mean." She broke down, her sobs tugging at my heartstrings. I hadn't learned enough about her to know an iota of what her life was like. But we all have our own lives to lead. "Please come down, Rion. I need you."

Mind racing, I figured it would take at least eight hours to drive there. Would a flight be possible? Probably, but not in my budget. I decided I'd drive.

No. On second thought, could I have bloodwork done locally? Probably. I called a clinic.

The more I thought about Courtney's situation, the more anxious and unsure I felt.

What would happen if the baby was mine? It didn't help to know there were other possible fathers. What would that mean for Dani and me? Would she stay or would I lose her? We were still so fresh in our relationship. And I didn't feel good about leaving Dani alone. Not now. Not with the continued harassment by her ex.

There was no denying my own egoistic worries. How awful would Dani think of me if she found out?

Was our connection based on love and trust? I snorted. Doubtful Dani trusted me, then again, perhaps I shouldn't assume. Courtney happened before I ever met Dani. I had opened up about not telling my family about my discharge, but to be fair, being honest about a lie of omission painted me in a poor light.

Those and a million other questions raced through my thoughts as I set out to find Dani.

I found her sitting in the bird enclosure, Snow cradled in her arms as she stared off in a daze.

"Dani?"

She startled. Her jump upset Snow, who squawked in irritation. Snow climbed up Dani's arm and perched on her shoulder, holding a leg out for me to pick her up. I obliged and stroked the soft feathers, like luxurious, cool fabric, against my fingertips.

Timsy and Fleur were quiet as if they sensed the chaos of our thoughts and didn't know how to soothe us. Snow, the introverted empath, insisted cuddles would heal everything.

"Dani," I began, but she cut me off, holding her hand up.

"Not around the birds, okay?" She asked, her voice barely above a whisper.

I should have taken the time to gather my thoughts, but they were too scattered, like a herd of cats in a room filled with a rotating disco ball.

Instead, I focused on the bird until Dani was ready to go back inside.

"Will you go with me?" I asked. Once we were back in her room, I shared my plan to call a local clinic.

Dani crawled beneath the covers and turned away from me. "No. I think this is something you need to face on your own."

"Dani, trust me. I don't believe it's mine."

"Until you know for certain, it's best we take a break." Her voice faltered at the end.

Her sad response was like a punch in the gut. "Dani, I can't just walk away from you," I said, unable to mask my frustration.

"Sure you can. You stayed away from your family, and I'm sure you love them." Her laugh sounded like shattering glass. "I was alone before you arrived. You were, too. Nothing will change now."

No words came out after I opened my mouth. I was choking on them, suffocating beneath the pressure of Courtney's accusation and what felt like Dani's rejection. An ache settled behind my left eye, the pressure building with each passing second and I found thoughts hard to piece together.

"So you want me to leave?" I asked, my mind swirling and my throat feeling tight. "What are you trying to say?"

She gave a deep sigh, and her anguish was clear in her voice. It wrapped around my heart and squeezed tight. "I don't know. I don't want you to leave, but you need to sort out the situation with Courtney." Her shoulders trembled, and the air seemed to be sucked out of the room. "Once that is done, we can talk."

"Dani." My voice broke as my world fell apart around me.

I walked around to the other side of the bed. She was crying, and each tear felt like a bullet to my chest.

"You are welcome to stay out at the cottage until you know for certain."

Damn it.

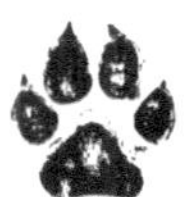

I called Elliot to alert him to the recent call from Darius and ask if they could get Dani to go somewhere else.

Elliot made a noncommittal noise. "Yeah. I doubt we can get Dani to leave. Dad suggested we have a couple of officers do surveillance."

Undercover, out of sight. Give her peace of mind while not bothering her.

"That's not a bad idea. She has the next three days off," I offered. Then I broke my news. Kinda. "I might need to leave for a couple of days, though. I have some shit I gotta take care of."

"Oh? Why doesn't she go with you?"

I rubbed my head. My hair had grown out to where it now curled. "She would rather not."

"Orion? You two good?"

What an intuitive bastard. "Not really. No. Something came up, and it caught me, both of us, off guard."

"I'll talk to her. Don't worry. We'll keep an eye on her. Get your life straightened out. But do it for yourself, not for Dani. She doesn't need any more baggage."

No truer words had been spoken in my life.

FOrTY-TWO

DANI

I watched Orion's Bronco roll down the drive and wondered where he was headed and if Thor tagged along.

How stalker-ish would I be to stroll to the beach and swing by the cottage to check?

I drop my forehead to the plane of glass I'd been staring out of for the last hour. My breath fogged the glass in an incrementally expanding circle, assisted by my also incrementally heavier exhales.

Straightening, I swiped my index finger through the condensation.

LOSER

Me and my awesome inside voices. With companions like them, I sure didn't need the violent ex-husband memories or his new harassment. Then again, many of my inner monologues featured his voice-over.

Sadness. So much misery and gloominess and for once, I knew the reason.

Sadness wasn't a choice. Love was a choice. Actions were choices. Acting on feelings were choices.

In my experience, I couldn't choose to not be sad. I could choose actions that distracted me. The brain puts out its chemicals, in the "correct" amounts or not. Sure, some therapies help. Positive affirmations. Learning appropriate coping skills—no, not drinking.

I sipped on a glass of red wine.

Hooking up with him was a choice I refused to regret, although this ache was an unfortunate side effect that I predicted.

"You're trouble," I said to the window.

Sending him away was a choice. My mental lull... not so much a choice but a product of a severe lack of Orion, or my lust and attraction to him. Those baffling brain chemicals.

On top of everything, the sun was shining and the beautiful ocean was slapping the beach playfully. If only the weather could have the decency to match my mood. Cloudy gray skies, maybe a fog or heavy mist would be great with the occasional fork of lightning.

Several official-looking men had already visited and updated the security system, even adding motion detectors to trigger ground lights all around the property. I stayed up much too late the night before watching the yard go off like lame fireworks as large night bugs, bats, and a raccoon triggered them.

Thanks to insistence on staying on the property, my parents hired teams to check in often, disguised as repairmen and such. To me they looked like exactly what they were—sentinels.

I stepped away from the window. The ocean's relentless call won me over and I grabbed a paperback and searched for my water bottle that I thought I had left outside the bird enclosure. All the stress was getting to me, leading to forgetfulness. I finally found it on the bench near the hot tub, somewhere I hadn't been lately that I could recall. Then I headed down to the ocean.

Thor was not in the cottage, much to my disappointment. If I stayed in the cottage for more minutes than necessary so I could fill my lungs with Orion's air, so what? Except, I felt eyes on me the entire time.

En route to the ocean, a plain clothes cop playing the role of a groundskeeper followed me at a distance. If you didn't know to look, he blended into the landscape well enough. The increased number of cameras in and around the house as well as the tailers were making me paranoid.

Remembering an oddity from earlier, I sent a text to my mom. *Can you please remind them not to touch or move my things?*

I believed that ensuring the teams my folks paid good money for had explicit orders to not move my things as they did their rounds would ease my mind.

Mom responded with, *Of course. Doni!*

I inhaled deeply, sucking in the sea air before slowly releasing it for a count of four. Everything I couldn't do because of the increased monitoring, and not necessarily things I have done or wanted to do, crossed my mind. Like masturbating on the beach—sandpaper fingers anyone? Burping and farting in the house or the yard. Scratching my butt. Staring off into space for hours on end—it makes people nervous you might be having a fit. Shaving my cooter and other unmentionables at the kitchen sink, because let's face it, the kitchen garbage can has the perfect dimensions to set beneath me with my one leg propped on the sink. At least I could still pee in the shower.

I kicked off my shoes, dropped the heavy water bottle, and jogged down to the water. The surf rushed at my feet, stealing my breath with its chill. A long vacation somewhere tropical would be better. Or Iceland. For several months.

I chuckled at my wry wistfulness. There was no way in hell I could leave my job for that long.

Besides, Darius had more patience than we ever gave him credit for. He might harass me for years. The sobering thought sat like a cold stone in my belly. Keeping Orion away ensured his safety, right?

Thinking of Darius brought me further down. He excelled at that effect. Perfected it and all because of consistent effort.

Funny how memories can trigger emotions. Compounded with my recent actions of evicting the *one* person in my life who made me laugh *and* orgasm, well, it knocked me down hard on my ass.

To get my mind elsewhere, I ran through the neurochemical reactions that fueled my desire. Nothing like science to set one's head on straight.

Oxytocin—one culprit for my missing Orion.

But that would be starting near the end.

In the beginning, lust came first. One could argue attraction took front and center, but I'm starting with lust. I thought he was hot, imagined what he covered with his gray sweatpants, and admired his muscles and strong features. Lust.

The water pushed and pulled at me where I sat, foam frothing across the sand. I leaned forward into my knees, holding my book up out of the water between my knees and chest. The wind tugged strands of my hair free from the fishtail braid. I closed my eyes against the assault of hair and spoke softly, needing to hear words aloud.

"Lust triggers the release of estrogen and testosterone. These hormones stroll through the brain and turn off the lights in rooms that regulate critical thinking and rational behavior. It makes us dumb." I laughed. "They also stimulate the release of dopamine and norepinephrine, the feel-good chemicals that get the heart pumping. They made women giddy, energetic, and euphoric. We eat less and have more sleepless nights because of them."

Finding him handsome and he, in turn, saying the right things and touching me in magnificent ways, was like a Pavlovian bell, a reference trigger for a cascade of reactions in my body.

Neurochemically, attraction affects the brain's pathways for reward behavior. In essence, "love struck." Although, one could also view me as a dog in heat.

The tide was going out, otherwise, I would be in danger of ruining my book. A rogue wave could still damage it, but I didn't have the energy to move. The heat had left my body and my limbs were numb. This bitch was glum.

Gah, I've hit rock bottom and started rhyming.

To me, attraction always seemed a softer emotion. Not gentler than lust, but more moony and backhanded to the forehead-type of swoon.

I continued building the flowchart in my mind. *Touch stimulates the peripheral nervous system, which triggers the hypothalamus to produce more testosterone and estrogen.* An image of Hans and Frans popped into my head. "They *pump you up.*"

Continuing, I increased my volume, the words carried away by the breeze. "Estrogen promotes dopamine release and a different high. Next comes arousal and its release of nitrogen oxide and noradrenaline. Pupil dilation, racing heart, increased respiration. These substances also increase blood flow and enlargement of the labia and lubrication."

My recital and memories of Orion had triggered the same pathways I was describing as a way to *not* think about him. I paused my speech to the ocean. Ever the captive audience, it splashed me in response, bubbles gathering and snapping around me as a reminder that it, too, had a hand in wetting me.

"Fine," I grumbled and continued on. "Orgasm is a release of oxytocin. That hormone induces rhythmic muscle contractions. The larger the release of oxytocin, the more intense the experience. The conscious altering big O is provided by Oxytocin." I dipped my head in acknowledgment of that fine drug.

I recalled oxytocin being called the *cuddle* hormone as it's also released during breastfeeding. Breastfeeding made me think about having a baby. Having a baby made me think of Courtney and killed my teeny, tiny happy buzz.

Continuing, I kept my mouth shut and thought, *After an orgasm, the body is rewarded with a surge of dopamine, something I'm currently lacking.*

A sad sigh worked through my body, ripe with darkly sour anxiety and I shivered. All chemical reactions... not love.

Love wasn't the heart-thumping response.

Love was a choice, not a feeling.

How unpoetic.

My neck prickled like someone was watching me. I glanced behind me and at the rocky cliffs of the cove but saw no one. A sailboat, sails up and tight, traveled some distance out, far enough that I could pinch it with my fingers. Whoever captained that beauty needed binoculars to spy on me.

The day was perfect for sailing. Less perfect for sulking.

"Face it, Danica Lavigne. Sending him away was a choice. And you regret it."

I agreed with my words wholeheartedly. Especially knowing deep down he understood and supported me. Protected. He made me feel safe.

Unlike Darius, who threw out so many red flags even though I had been too love blind to see or too needy to care, Orion's flags were a secure and strong yellow. Thanks to ongoing therapy and treatment, surer footing supported his shaky mental ground, like hard-parked earth over a fault instead of a bridge made of disintegrating, thin wood planking suspended across a mile-long gap over a bottomless canyon. I hoped speaking with his parents gave him a reprieve from the guilt and anxiety.

If I was going to be honest with myself, the Courtney affair wasn't a deal breaker. Even as I closed my eyes and thought about tomorrow, Orion playing with a faceless child and an older Thor on the beach slipped into my mind as easily as sliding into a hot tub.

Yes, he needed time to sort out doctor visits and potentially a lawyer for counsel, which was why I justified sending him away. I worried he would leave me anyway, duty-bound to care for a woman and unborn child. He claimed his time with her had been a fling, but I couldn't shake the doubt that gathered like a flock of gulls for a carcass washed up on the sand.

I wanted to hear his voice but feared his rejection.

Standing, I fought the chills that had set in deep. I tried to jog to my shoes, but couldn't, my legs were stiff and uncooperative.

When I eventually made my way back to the house, Orion's Bronco was sitting in its parking spot. I slunk back to my house for a hot shower and the rest of the bottle of red wine.

I should have known something was wrong the moment I stepped into my house. At first, I thought little of it, expecting that it was just me being paranoid. But as I moved through the house, it became more and more clear that something was off.

My favorite blanket draped over the back of the chair in a way that I would never have left it. The pillows were arranged in a single neat line, instead of two on each end of the couch. It was almost as if someone had been in my house, moving around my things.

I shivered involuntarily, feeling my anxiety rising, and I hugged myself tight. I still felt as if I was being watched, and the feeling of unease was overwhelming. I wanted someone to talk to, someone to tell me that I wasn't just being paranoid, that something had actually happened. One of the hires had tried to tidy up, or Orion stopped by just to check on me.

I went around the house, checking to see if anything else was awry. Everything seemed to be in place, but when I removed my earrings and tossed them in a cup on my dresser, they clinked against another piece of jewelry. My wedding ring. That I kept in a ring box, taped shut.

Pawning it had been my plan since before I left Darius. The sickening drop in my stomach triggered a violent and overwhelming fear. I wanted to believe that it was nothing. I wondered if someone was still in the house, but I knew I was alone. The monitors would have sent me an alert and the officers on watch would have come to investigate.

I shivered again, feeling a chill run down my spine, and I decided that it was time to leave. I quickly gathered my things and hurried out the door, closing it tightly behind me.

Once outside, I took a deep breath and tried to calm my racing heart. I felt like my paranoia had been justified, that something was indeed wrong. But I had no proof. I would just have to wait and see what I could find out.

FOrTY-THree

ORION

My mom called and asked us if she and Dad could come for a visit.

"Honestly, Rion, I need to get out of this icebox."

"Yeah, Mom. That would be great. Let me check with Dani on dates. I'd rather you got to meet her when you were here." There was no way I was going to let them know about my current troubles, although I could use some words of comfort. Instead, I held my secrets close.

Oblivious, she said with a wide smile, "Please do. Send me a text with dates that will work."

I nearly broke, needing to remind myself every action has consequences. I needed to face mine head on.

A clinic about fifteen minutes from Dani's scheduled me for blood-work. Courtney was not happy I wasn't coming down, but she provided her information.

Realizing I was probably being an ass, I said, "Look. We are not a thing, Courtney. I am not trying to be a dick, but you need to understand where I stand. I will take responsibility if it's mine. When we get the results, we'll need to talk more."

I held on to a tendril of hope that my infertility was still present. In fact, I requested a semen evaluation for the present. Would it be so bad if I knocked Dani up? Considering how fast the elation struck with the thought, I allowed myself a few moments to think about what our kid would be like.

My dream took a nosedive when I realized I did not know what Dani felt about kids. Her hectic life might not be what she wants to bring a family into. I did not know.

I decided to not go down that road with its topsy-turvy path.

Thor and I were stuck in the cottage together, though neither of us felt much like talking. Incredibly lonely, I had the test to look forward to at the clinic.

The cottage smelled like Dani. The bedsheets retained hints of her lotion and notes of vanilla, patchouli, and sandalwood mingled with lime, orange, and musk. God, I was analyzing her scent. She wasn't a bourbon or wine to flavor, yet her essence clung to me as powerfully as my need for her.

No matter how much I tried to keep myself together, anxiety flooded my veins at the prospect of the tests that waited for me at the clinic. How the results would affect my relationship with Dani.

Before I met her, I regularly spent time alone. Never lonely. I enjoyed my freedom.

Now, though, I felt isolated. Detached. Dismissed. Discharged. Unwanted.

A humorless laugh tumbled out of me. Apparently, I was also a thesaurus.

That first night, I spent hours in a dreamless sleep. Thanks to the winners of modern medicine, I woke up with a start when the sun rose. My mouth was dry, and I felt the weight of Thor's head on the pillow beside me.

Thor's.

Not Dani's.

My skin was hot, and my heart pounded like a jackhammer. I tried to swallow but could not. A sense of dread filled me, as if there was a demon in the room with me, hiding in the dark.

I scooted from my warm bed and sprinted down the hallway, skidding to a stop in front of the bathroom. My stomach clenched and I wretched and vomited an acrid stream into the bowl until there was nothing left inside me. Yet still the waves of nausea came crashing down, my body shaking as I clung to the cool porcelain of the toilet bowl, my cheek pressed against it until I could find the strength to stand again.

Every other minute I peered out the window, hoping I'd see Dani making her way across the yard to the cottage. I wanted to call. Text. I was driving myself insane.

The ocean was a powerful force later that morning, pushing and pulling against me with each wave. I felt my heart pounding, my vision blurred, and my chest tightened. I started pacing back and forth in the sand, feeling like I couldn't sit still no matter how hard I tried. Thor felt my distress and began pacing with me, nudging me with his nose and staying close by my side. It was almost like he knew I needed him to help keep me safe from the strong currents of darkness gathering around my edges. Luckily, the tide was going out, otherwise, it would have swept me away in the strong surf.

The fear of the test results wasn't as unbearable as the waiting. It hung over me like a dark cloud, threatening to burst at any moment. And yet the cruelest torture was Dani's silence. I wanted to bend, to break the silence.

Instead, I gave her space.

I gritted my teeth and tried to keep my composure as I went through the bloodwork and reproductive exam, counting the moments until I might be relieved of the unknown.

The doctor had a tech pull of blood before he left me alone with lube and a cup gut me to collect a sample of ejaculate. And had a tech draw blood. She referred me to a male infertility specialist but went over different treatment options, such as a vasoepididymostomy-expialidocious. Not that I was in a rush, but as I was in the beginning of the third decade of life, I had a sudden urge to discover the extent of my current reproductive health. "We can aspirate fluid here from either or both your testicles and epididymis to gauge potential fertility and determine the proper treatment. But I wouldn't have time today. You'd have to schedule another appointment."

The severity of my disjointed mental state broke through and I had a moment where I damn near lost it, thinking of Dani cleaning those geldings' wankers. The doctor noticed my near distress, so I told her the story and that I'm thankful for opposable thumbs and first-world hygiene opportunities.

At first, she didn't believe me, but I insisted, "Not making it up, doc. I watched my girlfriend, a veterinarian, perform the cleaning. Horses can't lick themselves like dogs."

She huffed a laugh. "I guess not."

She promised results within hours for the semen eval. "The DNA test will take two to four days. With the weekend coming, I would expect to be in touch with you no later than Wednesday next week. This Friday at the earliest."

A few more days to wallow. Later the same day, I met with my counselor and she talked me through my situation. Praised me on my progress and taking charge of my health. The bottom line, she helped a little.

I finally broke down and called Mom.

"I'm struggling, Mom. More so than after my injury."

"Have you talked to her since she asked you to leave?"

"No. Day before yesterday was the last time I saw her."

"You should at least send her a message. She's going through a tough time, too. The least you can do is let her know you are thinking of her."

"You think that would be all right?" I hated how weak I sounded. "I don't want to badger her." Although I hadn't shared Dani's past with my mom, it was constantly on my mind lately.

"Yes, dear. She'll let you know if she wants more from you. I'm so sorry you are going through this, but we are here for you. Let me know if you need anything or just want to talk."

"Thanks, Mom. I love you."

I heard her sigh. "Oh, I love you, too, Orion. Be safe."

I typed out text after text, deleting them because they were corny or just sounded lame until I finally decided on one that didn't sound like a dumbass wrote it. *Hey. Thinking of you. Thor misses your full-body massages.*

Three dots immediately appeared, showing Dani was typing a response. *Just Thor?*

I typed: *I miss u 2*

How much? Use your words, big guy.

I called her. "So fucking much, baby."

Her voice quavered with emotion. "I miss you too."

"Can I—"

"Will you—"

We spoke simultaneously, then laughed.

"Please come back," she said.

"Back where, baby?"

"Home."

Before I could, I had to check in with the plainclothes cops. They questioned me, checked my ID, played with Thor, and then escorted me to the back of Dani's.

After two dark, dismal days, I felt like I could breathe again.

FOrTY-FOUr

ORION

The next few days flew by quickly. The PI confirmed Darius was at his home in Wisconsin. Dani relaxed and her parents called off the hourly watch, but the cops continued their frequent stops. I think they enjoyed Thor and the birds.

Dani apologized for how she reacted after Courtney's call.

"Seriously, I don't blame you. You took it better than I might have." The clinic called and confirmed I was sterile, at least for that specific sample. I shared that I still had about zero chance of getting her knocked up and that I wasn't the only guy in the running. "Still waiting to hear if Courtney's child is mine."

"Well, I'll be here to help however I can."

"There are some tests I would like to have done to see if my sterility could be reversed."

"Oh?" She gave me a shy smile. "You're thinking you would like to have kids?"

I shrugged. "Definitely someday." Not wanting to scare her, I asked, "What about you? Ever want to have kids?"

She grinned and held up four fingers. That got my eyebrows raised.

As soon as I processed the number, an image of Dani and me with four kids playing on the beach popped into my head. I glanced at Thor who had rolled onto his back for a belly rub. With his mouth agape and tongue hanging near his wide and wild eye, he appeared as excited about the concept as I felt.

Until the future arrived with such a possibility, I decided to wing it and enjoy my time with Dani.

Open and honest. Two things Dani insisted we held high on our list of important things to be. This didn't mean we shared every detail of secret missions or the number of sexual positions with each ex, thank God.

It meant... How were we feeling? What issues did we face?

For example, when she came home exhausted, she told me. Bluntly, although not unkindly. More often than not, I instinctively knew when she needed me, her big dick, holding her rather than an hour of sleepless stuffing.

That meant I had to describe my boners—sorry to sound like a thirteen-year-old boy. I explained my erections resembled the tide. Once it rose, it wasn't going down soon. And like the tide, it, er he, responded to the moon.

My moon.

Her.

Ahh. I know she gave up fifteen minutes of precious sleep for that explanation.

She claimed I bred like a rabbit, often and, occasionally, quickly. I performed with speed rarely, thank the stars, although I ensured to tend to the moon's garden.

That, apparently, made me a weirdo. No, not the giving her an orgasm part. That I called her sexy parts *her garden*. It made her laugh. I loved making her laugh. Loved hearing such a carefree, happy sound.

And it dawned on me with the subtle sweetness of a sunrise... I loved her.

An uneasy shadow hung over her at the beginning of my return. She insisted it wasn't me, just her dwelling on maladjustment from evicting me earlier. In turn, I insisted we start over with a clean slate. And like her entire soul breathed a sigh of relief, she relaxed.

After everything, I convinced her to request some time off so we could get away.

Luck smiled upon us and her boss granted her a leave of absence, so we hit the beaches down south as well as Magic Mountain.

She invited her good friend and colleague, Katey Best, to join us, but due to her own work obligations, she managed only to provide a place to stay and two nights of company at her bungalow. Katey also offered a place for Thor to hang out while Dani and I unleashed ourselves on every roller coaster at least once.

The rush of heart-pounding drops, gut-twisting turns, and one minor fainting episode on the Goliath meshed well with candied apples, sugary lemonade, and blistering sunburns of our day excursion to Magic Mountain. For those several hours, we lived high and free from doubts and worries.

Later that night, we hung out at Katey's. A year older than Dani, Katey Best had a vibrancy that made me anxious. Vivacious and muscular with a shit-eating grin a mile wide, I presumed the woman was not one to pull her punches. Not without merit, I should add. Dani shared Katey had swooped in and rescued her at her lowest moment.

I would forever be in her debt, for without Katey and her efforts at supporting her friend, who knows if Dani's vehicle would have struck mine that fateful early morning?

Butterfly effect.

Purchased right before a housing crisis when prices were at an all-time low, Katey lived in a small, two-bedroom in an Armenian neighborhood in Burbank. With a high redwood privacy fence around the property and multiple live oaks, palms, citrus, other greenery, and a pergola—held up more by wisteria and bougainvillea—the place offered a serene escape from the chaos of the metropolis.

I'd give it a ten even for the location and limited running space. She had installed an electric deterrent at the top of the fence to prevent any baddies from sneaking into her yard to hide from search choppers.

Her only companions were a large, overweight orange tabby and a tank of saltwater fish.

"How is it you burned your shoulders so bad?" Katey wrinkled her upper lip as she handed Dani a bottle of after-sun lotion. "You're already tan."

Even through the fiery kiss of heat, Dani still blushed as she shook the bottle of relief.

I said, "Here. Let me take care of you."

Katey hummed and crossed her arms as she leaned against the doorframe. "So eager. The question of the night, besides the burn," Katey directed a pointed look to Dani before turning back to me, "is if you, Orion, are a good idea?"

"Katey," Dani admonished, then hissed, the cool lotion apparently a shock to her system. "Be gentle."

Whether she meant the request to me, Katey, or both of us, didn't stop me from my goal of making her more comfortable. Why hadn't I suggested sunscreen? Oh yeah, because I never burned.

I placed a light kiss on Dani's cheek, carefully lightening my touch to little more than a skim across her skin leaving a thick smear of aloe vera, lavender oil, and rosemary, a pleasant ingredient to burnt flesh. My dilemma became how to rub the balm into her shin.

I proceeded with extreme caution.

Her forest green eyes looked down when Dani said, "I use tinted body lotion, alright? Happy?"

My eyebrows lifted. "Really? That's why you don't have a tan line?" Here I imagined her sunbathing in the nude on the beach or beside her hot tub.

She huffed a laugh, winced, and said, "Yeah. In all my spare time."

When I finished, she turned to Katey, planting her back to my front. My body flushed and reacted to her proximity as per usual. Thankfully, she blocked my rise to attention.

Not now, boy. Our girl is hurting.

I rested my hand on her hips and my chin on her head as she spoke, feeling the low timbre of her voice in my chest. She rested her hands on mine and made a slight adjustment with her ass, triggering a zing of electricity through my eager dick.

She would be the death of me, or Katey would if I messed up.

"Orion is a wicked man who intended to steal my virtue repeatedly, but I beat him to the punch and stole his," Dani said.

Katey quirked a dark eyebrow. "But will you be good to my baby girl or will I have to dig a hole in the desert?"

I offered Katey my hand to shake, not leaving my post supporting my girl. My dick wouldn't allow it. "I'll help you dig if I manage to fuck anything up. You have my word."

Her coffee-colored gaze skipped between Dani and me. "He knows?"

Dani's head bobbed, her hair a gentle brush over my neck.

"I know enough about her ex. And she knows enough about my demons."

Thor rose from where he lounged on the heritage oak floor and stretched.

Katey swooped down and hefted Thor into her arms. He rewarded her by washing her face, going for the eyes. What was it with him and mascara?

"Okay, then. I ordered delivery for a half from now. Let's grab some beers and head out back."

Dani and I followed, ready to get off our feet.

For several days, local and national meteorologists forecasted extreme weather for the coast. Alerts popped up on every social media outlet and emergency text alerts. Torrential rain, dangerous winds, high surf, possibly hail. Touted as the Storm of the Decade, we planned to be back home to wait it out, unless evacuations became a requirement.

As the front approached the coastline, Dani and I watched the massive rolling cloud formation from the safety of the screened-in deck of her home. Lightning forked within and below the hefty front and created a mesmerizing silhouette of the cottage. The surf pounded the beach, roaring like a wild beast from hell. Although a stupid wish, I wanted to be out on the beach, but the energy coming off the water was intense at the house. To experience the thrill of the roiling water called to my soul.

"The way you describe things, Rion, makes me think you should try your hand at writing."

Dani's weird like me from my musings. "Writing? What, like novels?"

She nodded.

"Ha."

"Don't laugh. What if we wrote one together? Just for fun?"

A bright light flashed to the north.

Writing was one of those creative venues that I used to consider pursuing after reading a particularly great or extremely horrid novel. Lately, I followed Lindsey's advice and put pen to paper to get shit out of my head. I wish I could write something memorable. Having perused Dani's extensive collection of stories, I wondered what kind of book she would want to write. "I've seen your bookshelves. You need to dust more. There are a lot of dirty books on your shelves."

She held a hand over her mouth and mock-gasped. "Whatever do you mean, sir? You make it sound like *dirty* is a bad thing. "

"Dirty is a very, very good thing, in my opinion. That one story," I rattled off a romance title, "was more detailed than Penthouse Letters."

"It's not the details, baby, but the storyline attached to them. Besides, I bet you enjoyed reading that novel."

"Kidding me? I read three other books by the same author. Your idea has merit. But at the moment, I could use my fingers in a better way." Then I attacked.

She shrieked with laughter as I tickled her. The sweet sound would forever cause a release of my own endorphins.

A boom sounded overhead, our beer bottles rattling on the glass table-top. The incoming storm looked to live up to its forecasted intensity.

Panting, she blew a lock of hair from her face. Her cheeks held a rosy glow from the exertion and the roller coaster outing. Her shoulders were peeling, but no longer painful.

"We should go inside."

Lightning forked and laced brilliant patterns in the clouds and, while I would have preferred to watch them, Thor's terror of the storm and our safety became the priorities.

She picked up the empty beer bottles while I grabbed and pocketed the bottle opener, a multi-tool of sorts she picked up at some vet conference. Then I reached for a cowering Thor, who without a spot he made behind me, had crawled beneath the bench. Once inside, he wiggled, wanting to chase after Dani, so I put him back down.

No sooner did the door latch than the rain pounded down. We checked on the parrots and found them safely tucked inside their room, snoozing.

Although he wanted to play, soon the thunder overwhelmed Thor. He trailed me, stumbling into my heels.

We decided the best way to pass a storm was to watch a movie. I grabbed a couple of sodas from the fridge and nestled in with my girl on the couch. She drank from a beer bottle.

"We forgot these inside. I must have opened them before we went out back."

"Best not waste them," I said, not really wanting another. I took a swig and wiped my mouth on the back of my hand. For sitting out while we were watching the storm, it seemed pretty cold. A bit on the skunky side, too.

Dani scrunched her face after she took a drink, evidence her beer was off. We set them on the coffee table and settled into each other as we stretched out on the couch. Thor tucked himself between our legs and fell asleep.

The officers still making stops at Dani's place had checked in before the storm hit, so we looked forward to an evening free of interruptions.

Oddly enough, I dozed to the symphony of the thunderstorm and the entertaining sarcasm of Deadpool.

FORTY-FIVE

DANI

Waking came harder than an orgasm on antidepressants, even with the not-so-gentle slapping.

I tried to push Orion off me, but my arms seemed cemented at my sides. My mind whirred, halting with whatever dregs of sleep that refused to leave.

"Stop," I groaned after a particularly hard palm to my cheek that made my teeth throb.

"Wakey wake, Dani-girl. It's my turn to have some fun."

My insides iced, freezing all attempted motion or thought.

Darius.

Darius was here.

No.

No no no.

I was dreaming, I thought. Having another nightmare. I sucked in a lungful of air and tasted a familiar cologne, one that used to excite me, back before it linked itself with bitter ridicule and abuse. Now it made bile burn its way up my throat.

No nonononono. Wake up!

My skin tingled after another hard thump to my cheek. A fist.

It took a herculean force to open my eyes, and when I focused on the blurry face leering at me, I wanted to scream. Shout. Cry. Move. Anything.

But I couldn't. I was immobilized, my mind dulled and my body incapacitated.

"Oh, right. You can't move yet. That's the drugs. Do you like them?" he sneered in a condescending way of his.

Blinking took so much effort.

Darius leaned back and clapped his hands together, then held his line finger to his lips. "Shhh. Don't want to wake your lover." His abhorrent smile cast serious doubt on Orion's condition.

I gasped and managed, "Please don't hurt him."

"No *hello, sweetheart? Darius, how I've missed you?*" He held his hands clasped in front of his chest and batted his eyes like some villain imitating a loving damsel.

What an asshole. A very thin asshole.

Since the last time I saw him standing across the street in front of the courthouse with a police officer at his side, Darius had lost a considerable amount of weight. Rumpled clothing hung heavy with rainwater over his thin frame. His thick curly brown hair had been shaved into a military cut. He had been harassing me. Stalking, too, apparently. Was the crew cut his way of emulating Orion? Mocking?

Why hadn't the investigator or the security team discovered or prevented this... whatever *this* was?

The piercing indigo stare was the same. Hard. Uncaring. At least when we were alone.

He could be so charismatic and friendly, kind, around observers, playing the doting husband and lover. His high IQ led him into teaching, a respectable career, but rocky mood swings and a supreme case of narcissism made him lose his job shortly after I graduated from vet med.

He blamed me.

In turn, I could blame his mental illness, but I refused to grant him leeway. Refused to remove the blame when he chose to hurt me. Darius failed to take care of himself, failed to take his medication as prescribed, which sent him into dangerous bouts of violence.

Against me.

And here we were again.

"I love the new dog." Darius dipped out of my view.

We were in my bedroom. My clothing soaked through to my skin. Why was I wet? Right. Darius. I eased my head to one side as my captor reappeared holding Thor behind the front legs. The poor puppy shivered and flinched as thunder boomed. Rain drummed outside.

"He'll be as fun to gut as your last one."

Lightning cracked outside, the flash brilliant and blinding. The bedroom lights flickered and went out.

"Well, how exciting. I'll light a few candles... It will make our reunion so much more romantic."

A jarring brilliant glow appeared—his phone's flashlight—and beamed about the room, cutting through the harsh darkness.

I didn't want to revisit his ideas of romance but had no idea what to do. What had he drugged me with? And how? "What did you give me?" I slurred.

He rattled off chemical terminology, my brain too slow to process in real-time.

Flunitrazepam "Roofies?"

He waved a hand and dropped Thor. I heard a solid thunk as the puppy landed, followed by scrambling. He snuck beneath my bed. Good. At least he got out of sight.

Fuck my life. "You're here."

"I've been here for a while. Damon needed a place to stay and since I had to go out of town for training..."

Damon. Darius's twin. Estranged twin, I thought, who lived in Maine.

I hadn't been paranoid or losing my damn mind. The relief was short-lived.

"We are divorced," I ground out. *With a restraining order*, I failed to add because obviously, that meant little.

"I might have signed the paperwork, Dani-girl, but we cemented our bond in blood."

My gut rolled as violently as the storm outside. Bit by bit, my body loosened, and I regained motion. When I moved too fast, an odd rainbow-like aura shadowed any illuminated areas, mainly Darius and the flicker of candlelight.

"How did you..." My words stuttered and went out. How did he get inside? Why was he here?

"Oh, that was easy enough. The cameras weren't nothing. When you lived at home, you avoided looking directly at them when you came home from work."

I remembered with revulsion. He put the cameras up when he started suspecting me of bringing people home.

"And getting the code was easy enough. The crew liked to stop here last and hit a bar on their way home. One day it was a lone technician, and I added a little something to his drink-i-poo. He had all the codes in a little pocketbook."

He had developed a taste for Roofies, it seemed. *What a twisted fucker,* I wanted to say out loud, but my mouth was failed to form the words.

Darius continued speaking. "And with my recent weight loss, I dressed up in a sports bra," he said with venom.

The hatred toward workout clothing, well, I had never understood. He claimed they were too revealing, but I refused to wear sweatpants and a sweatshirt to run and lift weights and instead quit going to the gym.

The man continued spouting off information like he had an endless supply of jelly beans. The thought sat heavy in my queasy stomach.

"Shorty shorts. Got myself a ponytail wig. Shaved my legs. You want to feel how smooth my skin is?" His sneer looked so basic on his gaunt face as if he truly couldn't produce a different expression.

Another splinter wave of icy fear spread down my spine and I shivered in cool, wet clothing. I prayed Orion was alright. If he still lived, there was a chance Darius might lose this vile game.

FORTY-SIX

ORION

In my nightmare, darkness cocooned me, and I couldn't find Dani. I called out over and over, but she did not answer.

So dark it was that I was uncertain if I walked or ran.

I jerked awake, chilled and sweating simultaneously. The lights were off, as was the TV. Rain poured down, and I heard the trees whipping against the siding.

Dani wasn't snuggled on my lap like she had been during the movie. She didn't answer when I called. Neither did Thor.

I pulled his body out and into my lap. Lightning flashed, a blinding light illuminating the living area for a split second before the thunder cracked and shook the house. In the afterburn, I realized several things. Dani's burnt orange minky blanket draped off to the side onto the floor. The nearby lamp lay on its side, partially covered by the aforementioned blanket.

Not like Dani to leave her blanket on the floor.

In the brief silence, my ears strained.

There. I heard... something. Whispering? A thud?

The hair on the back of my neck stood on end as I slowly rose from the couch, unsteady and disoriented. I moved with caution, half expecting a demon in this darkened house to jump out at me. The way I stumbled and walked into the couch, I would give the demon plenty of warning of my approach. The occasional flicker of lightning gave me glimpses of my path.

In the hallway, I tried to quiet my breathing, but it was no use; every step seemed deafeningly loud in this still space, ringing through what felt like a graveyard. Just when I thought perhaps I imagined the noise... there it came again: a muffled sound behind Dani's bedroom door.

I took an involuntary step back as tendrils of cold crept up my spine before I realized who it was... Dani. She wasn't mumbling. She was moaning.

I heard shuffling. The carpeting felt soft under my bare feet as I inched closer to the door, the wood of the door cool under my hand. I reached for the knob and twisted, pushing open the door.

What I saw in that illuminated room petrified me. Surrounded by candles, a man stood at the end of the bed, his arm extended with a brilliant, sharp light. *What the fuck?*

Dani sprawled on the bed, a dark shadow spreading out beside her. I inhaled but failed to pick up the coppery tang of blood. Instead, wet and body odor permeated the room.

My heart raced, and time seemed to slip into slow motion. She glanced over at me where I stood, stunned. Her eyes glistened in the dancing flashes of light.

"Look who finally joined the party. Dani-girl, care to introduce me to your friend?" The man's voice dragged out the word *friend.*

I recognized his voice after only hearing a few words over the phone.

While on my last mission, I knew who the enemy was. I just couldn't always recognize them on sight. They infiltrated the fighters, passing as brothers in arms, armed women and children, or dogs with bombs.

I saw my enemy before me then.

The man was taller than Elliot but thinner. Gaunt. Darius stared at me with indifference. He wore a baseball cap and his dark clothing dripped rainwater onto the floor. He leered at me. I meant nothing. A minor detail standing in front of his prize.

Light reflected off the gun he had pointed at me. One way or another, I would do whatever to protect Dani.

"What do you see in this guy? That he is the complete opposite of me. He's skinny... must be a runner. Short, dark hair, in need of a shave." The indifference in his tone screamed out his contempt. "Well, I'm finally here. We can take some time to be reacquainted, Dani-girl. Hello. I'm Darius. Dani-girl's husband."

"Ex-husband," Dani said, the venom thick in her words.

"Yes, well, we had a few issues. All we needed was a bit of counseling to get you sorted out, honey. But you blamed everything on me. It takes two to make a marriage."

"Darius, please," Dani leaned up on her elbows.

"Don't you fucking move." Darius lashed out with his empty hand, a sharp smack sounding.

Dani's head whipped to the side, and she fell back to the bed.

"Now. Why don't you introduce me to this man who has been staying in your home?"

Dani only shook her head.

I doubted he needed an introduction. "What's the point of this?" I edged closer a little every time he looked back at Dani. Thor had scampered beneath the bed, safely out of the way for now.

"The point? The point? To get my girl back. Make her see how much of a mess she left me in. I still love you, Dani-girl."

My god, this man had a void where his soul should have been.

"Stop. Calling. Me. That."

"Here now. I'll forgive you for your mistakes, but I'll have to dispose of your new friend. You understand—"

Dani cackled. The blow to her head must have made her delirious. Then again, maybe she saw this as her final act with this narcissistic asshole. "Now that you mention it, Orion is exactly the opposite of you. Kind. Considerate. Patient. Honest. Perfectly easy to love."

I got hung up on the word *honest*. Seriously, I could do a lot better. Then the words "easy to love" registered.

"Hmm." He cocked his head to the side, examining his prey. "I bet we aren't so different. Did he get you off, get you to make that adorable stuttering sound? Or do we differ in that regard, too?" Darius sneered. "Ya know what? I don't give a shit. How about I make him easy to mourn?"

Cold resolve rooted in my gut, and branched out to my extremities. We were in my territory. Dani was mine to love and protect.

I lowered my shoulder and rushed him. The gun went off next to my left side, a sonic snap leaving me deaf in that ear. The man was a solid wall of muscle. Fortunately, I had enough momentum to force him to the floor.

He bucked and rolled. The gun went sliding across the hardwood. I grabbed his arm as he went after it.

Dani reached over the side of the bed and grabbed the gun. Pointed it at Darius. He stood slowly, raising his arms.

"Whoa, there," he began, then lashed out, knocking the gun from her grip. It went flying again, and I rushed for it.

My hand closed around the grip when I heard a thunk, and then Dani moaned the word, "No." That single syllable was enough to fill me with icy dread.

My heart beat loud and fast in my ears. He laughed. Laughed and struck her again.

"Put the gun down. You won't succeed at being a hero." I heard the metallic snick of the hammer.

"I didn't show up unprepared for this visit. Again. Drop the gun. Kick it toward me."

I did as he commanded, momentarily considering kicking it hard.

"On your knees."

As I lowered myself, my eyes flickered to Dani, who continued to lie motionless on the bed. My anger resurfaced as I pulled the only weapon I had—the multi-tool bottle opener from earlier. I flicked the corkscrew out and fit it between the third and fourth fingers of my left hand.

"Hands on your head."

I raised my hands, hoping the multi-tool wasn't visible.

He approached me with a lewd grin. "Tell me, Orion. Did you think she loved you?"

This guy was a complete and utter psycho.

"She's a user. Wants everything without giving back."

The big bastard threw a punch at me. It connected with the side of my jaw, snapping my head back. I saw a bright flash as if lightning struck inside the bedroom. My eyes and nose watered. At least I could clench my jaw and roll with the punch.

Somewhere, someone was ringing a bell, and I saw a flash of white over my head. Darius staggered back.

I lunged, flying past Dani, who had stuck Darius with a pillow.

Once again, he landed on his back. I straddled his chest, pinning his arms to his sides with my legs. I landed a swift punch to his throat, and he went from pitching and pawing at me to heaving and clutching at his neck.

I dropped the bottle opener, wanting nothing more than to brutalize this lowlife for every wrong he had handed Dani. My vision blurred as I slammed my fists into his ugly face.

During my last tour, so many things occurred I had no control over. There wasn't an enemy I could see to retaliate during that last attack. My brother-in-arms was in pieces. I survived, but I could do nothing. I could do something now. Fight back. So I fought back. My desire to save Dani conquered any fear or reservations for my own life. I had control.

Bright light blazed in a wide swath across the room and I panted between hits. His head became loose and bounced.

"Orion. Stop!"

Someone shook my shoulder, and I roared, ready to throw the person off me.

"Orion!"

I recognized Dani. Dani was crying. Dani was alive.

The man beneath me was still.

I slumped off him and pulled her to me, my hands leaving bloody streaks on her clothing.

"Orion. Oh, my God. Orion? Are you okay? Fuck. Stupid question. I'm sorry." Dani spoke rapidly, breaking down into sobs. "I'm so sorry, Orion."

"Baby, you have nothing to apologize for."

My hands were numb, but I grasped Dani and held her close. Darius sprawled on the floor. I couldn't tell if his chest moved, not with my blurry vision.

I squeezed my eyes and buried my face in the crook of Dani's smooth, warm neck. Her pulse thrummed like a hummingbird against my nose.

Forty-seven

ORION

The rest of the night was nothing more than a hazy, garish trickle of time. Police swarmed in, the flickering red and blue lights of their rides outside a macabre pattern through the living room.

They wanted our statements, and we provided them the best we could. We were both numb, the reality of the situation sinking in like a stone. Thor clung to my side, shivering.

The paramedics eventually loaded Darius onto a stretcher, zipping his corpse away inside a black body bag. When they wheeled him out, I noticed life reentered Dani's dull gaze. She straightened even as devastation and grief flickered across her face. My girl was fierce, and I nearly chuckled over the memory of her slugging Darius with a pillow. Not the best of ideas when delivering my narration of the night to the officer.

Elliot and Eamon appeared as I finished with the officers. Dani's brothers were a godsend. Neither fawned over Dani, although they both embraced her and whispered encouragement in her ears. While I held Dani close, they contacted electricians to reconnect the power which Darius had cut. Elliot made coffee, then helped Eamon clean Dani's bedroom.

Dani pleaded with her brothers. "Burn the bedding."

They nodded solemnly and set to work without hesitation.

By that time, Dani's parents had arrived. This was not the first meeting with her folks that I imagined, yet here we were.

Dr. Gavin Lavigne and Ariadne Creswell were what I expected and not. As a lawyer, I figured Adriane would be on the phone arranging support for Dani. Perhaps she had already done so on the drive over. At four in the morning, he and Gavin pulled Dani into the kitchen and together they began cooking.

Thinking I was better off observing, I sat at the island. Gavin presented me with a fresh cup of coffee and a handshake, his no-nonsense grip as striking as his gaze. The imposing black man was my height, yet seemed larger than life. A giant bear dressed in a teddy bear's persona. Gray laced his short hair. A smattering of freckles covered his nose and upper cheeks.

"Thank you for taking care of our daughter," he said as I pulled the steaming mug toward me.

I gave a curt nod.

A brief smile lit up his face before it was gone. "This was not how I imagined meeting you."

I huffed and ran my hand over my hair, the side stubble and short top grounding me. Funny how a good haircut reminded me of who I was. A protector.

"You don't say much." It wasn't a question.

My cue to talk. "No, sir. I am glad to finally meet you. Dani has talked a lot about you and her mom."

Adriane slid in beside her husband and offered her hand with manicured nails polished with pink gel. She had a warm, firm grip and a warmer smile. "Yes. Thank you, Orion."

"Just Rion, ma'am," I corrected her.

"His friends and family call him that," Dani looked over at me. She smiled, and her radiant heat soothed the chill that had frosted my heart.

Adriane lifted an eyebrow. The expression so like Dani's, I nearly choked on my sip of coffee. "Please call me Adriane, not ma'am." She leaned forward and loudly whispered, "It makes me feel ancient."

"I would certainly not wish to make such a young woman feel anything but." I dipped my head in polite deference.

Dani walked around the island and slipped her arms around my neck. I closed my eyes, relishing her nearness, and kissed the smooth skin on the back of her hand. She moved away to pick up Thor, who decided he too wanted a hug. I pushed the stool next to me out for Dani, and she sat holding Thor like the big baby he was.

An officer approached, halting the relaxed conversation. "We are unable to find Mr. Cooper."

Cooper. Had I heard that name before? Dani leaned in to tell me he was one of the plainclothes officers that her parents had hired to watch her residence.

"Is it possible he assisted the deceased in entering our daughter's home?" Adriane asked.

The officer nodded. "Until we find him, all possibilities are on the table."

Gavin's brows dipped. "I thought we properly vetted him?"

Nodding absentmindedly, Adriane sighed softly. "Keep us posted."

Dani's arm contacted mine, and I scooted closer. I threw an arm around her, joining us. Thor tipped his head back against my chest and made a try for my chin with his tongue. He succeeded.

Adriane looked my way. "I doubt there will be any charges brought against you."

I felt a shiver go through Dani and I squeezed her shoulder.

California is a "castle doctrine" state, meaning you may defend it if someone breaks into your home. Dani and I did what we had to do. If I could have done anything differently... no. There was no time to dwell. Our external injuries would heal quickly. I prayed our internal damage would heal just as easily.

Outside, the rain continued to fall, although its intensity had lessened. No amount of water could wash away the bloodshed that night. I fought for Dani, and she for me. But far worse than the physical harm we endured dwelled inside us after Darius had taken his last breath. For me, it was a dark, horrific sensation that descended like fog, threatening to consume me in its depths.

Every time our eyes met, it seemed there was an unspoken exchange between us, one filled with regret. There was sufficient strength and courage for the two of us in her gaze.

Darius brought his fate upon himself. He deserved to be put down like a rabid dog, and at least I kept that stain from Dani's soul. What flashbacks would the night reignite, and how would they chip away at what we had worked on? Was our bond strong enough to hold?

While we each suffered the trauma of Darius differently, we would face the fallout together.

FORTY-EIGHT

DANI

Orion and I stood together and watched my parents drive through the front gate. Thor sniffed around the hedges; his attention snagged on a particular scent. The rain had settled the California dust and left behind a stark reminder that cleansings were attainable and realistic.

Fate handed me my cards and when my turn came, I was all in. Now, the game had ended, and Orion and I were left showing the same cards. What would I be dealt on the next hand?

I reminded myself, *One breath at a time, Dani.*

My hands shook as I opened the door. My glass resolve shattered when I crossed the threshold. The turmoil of the night ripped me apart, flooding my vision with a sea of tears. I had been helpless against him at first, overwhelmed with the shock of seeing Darius invade my home. Threaten Orion and my family. His violation weighed me down like an avalanche of bricks. Every emotion I'd ever felt with him struck me at once like lightning. Never had I known such raw powerlessness—my mind was blank, not knowing where to turn or what to do.

Not until Orion appeared like a vengeful angel, prepared to destroy the world to save me. Instead, he destroyed the monster.

I stumbled into the living room wanting nothing more than to crawl into a corner and hide from the world. But as I glanced around the room, my eyes fell on Orion looking worn and haggard. He had cleaned up, but phantom blood still stained his hands and skin.

The couch creaked as Thor crawled upon it and curled in on himself for a nap. My body was exhausted, but my mind whirred with anxious thoughts.

With measured steps, I moved towards him until we were face to face. The weight of everything that had happened descended upon us like a dense blanket of silence, and neither of us spoke. I struggled to comprehend what that night meant for our future.

I trembled as Orion's arms enveloped me. It was as if he sensed my need to fall apart and held me tightly, his embrace like an unbreakable shield of strength and protection.

At last, Orion spoke, breaking the silence. "We will get through this," he said, his firm voice slicing through the shadows of my heart. The soothing power behind those words made me think he was assuring me that no matter what happened next, he would stick by my side. The badgering question lingered: how long would it be until he reached the limit with his own internal demons?

His arms were warm around me as I let out the sorrows of the night in one long weepy embrace. He kissed away my tears and held me close, whispering words of love and reassurance between each soft kiss. His touch broke through the veil of my despair and for the first time since walking through my door, I felt something stirring inside me—hope that maybe we could make it to the other side of this terrible night.

"Tell me what you need, baby," he murmured against my lips.

The bitter taste of panic coated my tongue as I opened my mouth to speak. "Love me until I'm me again," I said, unsure if I even knew who "me" was anymore.

The love and understanding in his gaze swept away any doubt I had. Hope surged within me that perhaps we could get through this. He nodded, pulled me closer still, and gave me back a sense of strength.

DECEMBER

JANUARY

FEBRUARY

MARCH

APRIL

FOrTY-NINe

ORION

My name is Orion Indigo Windwalker, and I finally have a fucking clue what to do with my future.

I walked out the revolving glass door into the warmth of a mid-April coastal Cali day, official papers in hand.

Dani caught up to me, having to use the restroom before we left the bank.

It was eight months since I last exited a building carrying a hefty stack of documents. With a far different set of papers clutched in my grip, I stood tall. I was ready for the marathon of life, this time wearing a rucksack full of love and gratitude.

Sappy, I know. But honest-to-God's-truth.

Oorah.

My escape took me several hundred miles up the coast of California, far from my blood family in North Dakota. It was here, though, that I found my soulmate.

My Dani.

Her bright smile added fuel to the burning in my heart and we stepped off the curb together, hand in hand. We climbed into the Bronco, and I drove several blocks away to a quaint strip mall filled with boutiques, a vet clinic, a kitchen supply outlet, and a cupcake shop.

I pulled into an open space directly in front of MASH Cakes.

"What are you thinking, Rion?"

I looked over to see an angel haloed in the warm light. A slow smile stretched across my face, mirroring the angel's grin. "How much I love you."

She leaned over and kissed me. I tangled my hands in her loose hair, my mouth and tongue giving and taking from the woman who made me feel whole. Filled my half-empty cup until it overflowed with happiness.

"We have an audience," she murmured as I nibbled my way down her neck.

"Sick fuckers," I said.

She snorted and patted my groin. "You can wait a few more hours, mister."

A few more hours? I had waited two long weeks while out of commission for my nut reattachment. The surgeon cleared me earlier today, before our meeting with the bank.

"I am not sure I can wait that long, baby." The warm weight of her hand disappeared from the front of my jeans, and I groaned.

"You waited thirty-two years for me." She winked, her emerald eyes sparkling with mirth.

"And what a mess I was until you," I replied, nuzzling my face into the crook of her neck.

She pulled away and raised an eyebrow skeptically. "What are you talking about? You were never a mess."

I grinned at her, grateful for her words. My days weren't always easy, but I continued to work hard and stay in the present, in love with the most incredible woman. It was a much better option than allowing the past to creep in and dull the joyous edges of my life. Let's be real, though. Mentally, my options weren't always a conscious choice, but I continued my therapy, which helped.

Our families cheered as we walked into the cool, bright shop. Yes, our families. My folks made the trek to meet their soon-to-be daughter-in-law, although I hadn't asked yet. The ring was in my pocket, and her earlier groping nearly had me undone in multiple ways.

Thor bounced around us, sniffing and talking in his doggy way. Mom hugged me while Adriane pulled Dani into her arms. Then the moms switched and Dani's mom embraced me. "We are so excited for you to become part of our family." Her words were for my ears only.

So, Gavin had shared what I recently asked him... for his daughter's hand in marriage.

Adriane and I shared a conspiring smile before I turned and greeted the others. Dad. Gavin, Elliot and his wife, Ginger. Eamon and Camile. Their kids. My brother Jeremy, his wife Mia, and their boys. Kya's absence sent a pang of sorrow through my center, but she had sent her congratulations earlier, saying she would be there when she could.

Everyone had come for the grand opening of MASH Cakes.

Tomorrow, hopefully, we would celebrate our engagement.

Today, we would feast on cupcakes.

The store was full of images of a cross-eyed Weimaraner with a cupcake balanced on its nose. Dani chose Thor as a mascot and had a friend design the MASH Cake logo after him. Crisp colors of blue and white canvassed the open space. A long counter with a glass front took up one side of the shop. Customers could select cupcake flavors and watch the staff smash them with frosting and roll them into balls to be dipped in a candy coating. There were options for gluten-free and keto-friendly.

The shop catered to dogs as well, a nod to those veterans with canine companions. Near the checkout, we set up a spigot to fill recyclable paper dog bowels. Only one flavor decked out as a fully edible and frosted cupcake was available for the dogs. Thor insisted they were better than any other treat he had ever tasted.

Today only, the shop opened with our families manning the stations and serving free smashed cakes to military personnel and their families.

Tonight, I would ask Dani to be my wife. The future stretched out with an exciting, limitless stretch of possibilities.

FIFTY

DANI

I found it difficult to pick the best part of the day as Orion, Thor, and I walked along our strip of beach. The grand opening went smoothly. The donation box to help military veterans bulged. I finally met Orion's parents, Carson and Kira, in person. They were adorable. And Jeremy and his family were wonderful.

My emotions got the best of me several times and I had to duck to the kitchen to compose myself. Orion, not an outgoing sort of guy, shook hands and patted the backs of each and every military person who walked through the door. Surely, he would need time to decompress, or perhaps our quiet walk along the beach was exactly that.

He had been quieter than usual since we returned to the house. Tired probably. I certainly was after the excitement of the day. His appointment to clear him for extracurricular activities. The bank stamped their approval on our loan. The grand opening of our shop.

Inhaling the sea air, I wanted to scream and shout, but doing so would drain the last bit of energy reserves and I needed them for when we returned to the house.

Orion tugged on my hand, and I turned into him. I wrapped my arms around him and stood on my tiptoes to rub my cheek against his. His spicy masculine scent filled my lungs as I breathed him in. Mixed with the night and the ocean, it filled me with want.

Before I could act on my desire, he stepped away, his face serious. My gut twisted with worry, and I opened my mouth to say something. Words failed me as he dropped to one knee.

Was he hurt?

"Dani."

Something glimmered between his fingers. Waves lapped the beach at our feet and in the distance, I heard Thor splash closer.

Orion cleared his throat. "Dani, marry me."

I gaped at him, my mind blanking out all other thoughts as I stared down into his deep blue eyes. Was he really asking what I thought he was? My heart hammered in my chest as I realized the enormity of this moment. Marriage? Me, get married again? For a second it felt like everything around us had stilled and we were the only ones remaining on earth.

The setting sun cast a golden glow over his face and made Orion's hair shine like light glinting off a raven's feathers. He waited for me to answer, his expression hopeful and uncertain.

"I...Yes." The word broke free from my mouth before I could even think about it properly.

Grinning widely, Orion stood up and took my hand in his so that he could slide the ring onto my finger. His hands shook. "You've just made me the happiest man alive," he laughed softly.

Tears sprang to my eyes and trickled down my cheeks before I could stop them. Without looking at the ring, I threw my arms around him. "I love you, Orion Indigo Windwalker."

His kiss tasted of saltwater and desire, and I melted into it. The heat of his body pressed into mine as he deepened the kiss. Our tongues twisted together in an intimate dance, a need consumed every inch of me for him. Breathless and far from sated, he broke from our kiss. He lifted my chin so he could look into my eyes, a wild and fierce look had taken hold of him. "I love you, too, Danica Rose Lavigne," he whispered huskily against my lips before kissing me once again.

Ever since the day my vehicle struck his, I'd been falling in love with him a little more every day. He filled my life with his solid presence, possessing my soul and body. I knew no matter where I went or what I did, he would forever be my home.

THE END

About the Author

S E Davis is a veterinarian and advocate for werewolf health. She lives on the North Dakota prairie with her family and a Weimaraner who understands shifting into human form is unnecessary for being part of the pack.

To learn more about Sarah and her books, visit her at:
Instagram: @sarahdavisauthor
Facebook: @sarahdavisdvm
Goodreads:
https://www.goodreads.com/author/show/20506113.Sarah_Davis
TikTok: https://vm.tiktok.com/TTPdYcBMMf/

https://linktr.ee/sdavisdvm

Also by S E Davis

They Had Eyes of Silver

They Had Eyes of Gold
They Had Eyes of Fire (coming soon)
They Had Eyes of Ice (coming soon)

Kindle Vella

Hel's Hounds

Prey

They Had Eyes of Fire

Lost in Under

Grandma Birdie's Crochet for Vampires

Buckles

Greyson

Beneath the Thorns and Red Roses

As Sarah Davis

Inside Voices

Prey

9 798986 164489